Above
the
Zodiac

Above
the
Zodiac

ASTROLOGY IN JEWISH THOUGHT

MATITYAHU GLAZERSON

JASON ARONSON INC.
Northvale, New Jersey
Jerusalem

Translated from אין מזל—לישראל by M. Kalish
This book was set in 12 pt. Garamond by A-R Editions, Madison, WI.

Library of Congress Cataloging-in-Publication Data

Glazerson, Matityahu.
  Above the zodiac : astrology in Jewish thought / by Matityahu Glazerson.
    p.   cm.
  Originally published: Jerusalem : M. Glazerson. 1985.
  ISBN 1-56821-935-0 (alk. paper)
  1. Jewish astrology.   I. Title.
 BF1714.J4G56   1996
 133.5'946—dc21   96-52273

Manufactured in the United States of America. Jason Aronson Inc. offers books and
cassettes. For information and catalog write to Jason Aronson Inc., 230 Livingston
Street, Northvale, New Jersey 07647.

To elevate and remember the souls
of my honored parents
JULIUS and FAGEL SMOLLAN
May peace be upon them
and upon my beloved sister
LIEBA PEARL
who loved and shared her talent for music
with all for so many years in Johannesburg,
and in appreciation to the management, staff,
and voluntary workers and supporters of
SANDRINGHAM GARDENS
for their dedication and sacrifice in helping
the aged and infirm.

dedicated by
VICTOR JACOB SMOLLAN

Contents

Preface

The book *Above the Zodiac* has been written in the spirit of our previous works, whose purpose was to introduce the reader to those fundamental ideas within Judaism that would serve to enrich the reader's appreciation of this great tradition.

The modern-day seeker of spirituality often feels that he must look to sources outside of Judaism to discover the paths to knowledge, wisdom, and spiritual awakening that, in actuality, have deep roots within the Jewish tradition.

In the case of the science of astrology, upon encountering those outside sources, we have observed that they forego the deep, timeless context within which these ideas are preserved in their Jewish framework, and instead reduce this study to the art of prediction, for the manipulation of the material world.

Within Jewish literature, the source for the spiritual meaning of the astrological constellations is the *Sefer Yetzirah* (*The Book of Formation*), whose authorship tradition attributes to the Patriarch Abraham. The *Sefer Yetzirah* contains the mysteries of the creation of the universe. Many commentaries have been written to elucidate this text. Among those used in this book are the commentaries of Rabbi Saadia Gaon, Nachmanides, and the Gaon of Vilna.

We have also relied on other books that expound the mystical meaning of the Jewish time cycle, such as *Bnei Yisaschar,* by Rabbi Yisachar of Dinov; *Pri Tzadik,* by Rabbi Zaddok Hakohen of Lublin; and others, as indicated in the text.

Introduction

The Practice of Judaism and the Science of Astrology

In the *Code of Jewish Law* (vol. 1, ch. 179, v. 1), we find a prohibition against the consultation of one's astrological forecast. From Rabbi Solomon Luria's commentary on Maimonides, it is inferred that this prohibition is derived from the biblical injunction against divination. According to Nachmanides, however, the source of the prohibition derives from the positive commandment of the Torah, "Pure (whole) shall you be with the Lord your God."

Notwithstanding this prohibition, Rabbi Moshe Isserles (*Code of Jewish Law,* vol. 179, ch. 179, v. 2) hands down the decision that "one who has heard a forecast from a competent astrologer may take this information into account, and ought not act contrary to the astrological influences, because one must not rely on miracles."

The *Zohar* (vol. 3, 216) states, "From the time that the Torah was given to Israel, the Israelites were withdrawn from the rule of the stars and constellations; however, if one does not follow the ways of the Torah, he returns to be under the domain of these natural influences."

In the Talmud we find various statements regarding the influences of the astrological signs on the Jewish people. In Tractate *Shabbat* (129b) is recorded a prohibition against the medicinal drawing of blood on the third day of the week, being that on that day, the influence of Mars is dominant. (In the Romance languages, the name of the third day of the week is derived from the word Mars.) Rashi, in his commentary on the Talmud, explains that the prohibition is due to the fact that the astrological influence of Mars is associated with war, plague, and disaster.

In Tractate *Nedarim* (32a) it is stated, "Our Patriarch Abraham said to the Holy One, blessed be He, 'I investigated my astrological fortune and found that I am due to have only one child' (Ishmael)." The continuation of this conversation is found in Tractate *Shabbat* (156a), where God answers Abraham, "Release yourself from the influence of your stars, for Israel is beyond the constellations. Your ruling planet is *Zedek* (Jupiter), which appears in the West. Based on its influence you are not due any more children. I, however, will move the planet *Zedek* (Jupiter) to the East, so that you may father another child, as it is written, 'Who caused the illumination of *Zedek* to the East; may it be called on his behalf.'"

Nachmanides writes, "The edicts of the stars constitute the basis of the hidden miracles mentioned in the Torah. However, the Jew, through the power of his choice and through his walking in the way of the Torah, may rise above the astrological influences."

The holy Ari, in explaining the possibility of normal birth after seven months' pregnancy, states (*Likutei Torah,* 7), "During these months, the fetus develops in its mother's womb through the power of the seven planets, for the Blessed God gave into their hands the rule over all human attributes." On the basis of this, we may answer one of the questions that the unbelievers ask with regard to the plural form used in the biblical passage, "Let us make man in our image." This plural form refers to the storehouse of attributes that the planets impart to the developing fetus, each in its month. Therefore God told the planets, "Let us make. . . ."

Many rabbis through the ages had a deep knowledge of astrology. Among them are Rabbis Saadia Gaon, Shmuel Hanagid, Avraham Ibn Ezra, Levi ben Gershom Nachmanides,

Isaac Abarbanel, Isaac Aboab, Isaac Arena, and Shabtai Dolno (who, in his commentary on *Sefer Yetzirah,* quotes many ideas from the second-century work *Beraita de Shmuel Hakatan*).

Ibn Ezra, whose books on astrology are currently available, writes in his commentary on the Torah (Deuteronomy, ch. 4, v. 19), "It is well attested that each nation and each city is linked to a star that advises it as to its fate; Israel, however, has a great fortune in that God alone is its advisor, for Israel is God's portion."

Rabbenu Bachaya, in discussing the astrological influences (Deuteronomy, ch. 31, v. 16), writes, "When the sages state that Israel is above the constellations they do not mean that the constellations have no influence on Jews, for we find it often mentioned in the Talmud and the Midrash, 'His astrological fate brought this about'. . . ."

The meaning of this transcendence is that Israel is not placed under the absolute rule of the stars. This is due to the fact that the entire creation came about for the sake of the righteous. Therefore, just as an effect cannot be placed prior to its cause, the astrological influences cannot exercise absolute determination over the fate of the righteous. However, among the gentiles we find that each nation has its ruling stars; therefore it is stated by the wondrous science of astrology that Scorpio rules over the Ishmaelite nations, Sagittarius rules over Persia, Capricorn rules over the Palestinians, Libra (or Virgo) rules over Rome, etc.

In the Pesikta Rabbah and in the Midrash Tanhuma, we find homiletical reasons for the creation of the signs of the zodiac. The Pesikta states (ch. 4), "Why did the Blessed Creator create the universe during the month of Nissan (whose sign is Aries)? Because when God decided to create the universe, he told the Master of Darkness, 'Depart from me, for I wish to create the universe with light' (the sheep symbolized by Aries is white in color). Whereupon the Master of Darkness (whose sign is Taurus, the bull, who is black in color) asked, 'And after light, what will you create?' And God answered, 'Darkness,' the sign of the month of Iyar (Taurus). [And the conversation continues] 'After darkness, what will you create?' 'Twins (Gemini), for man is destined to see through both light and darkness, and Gemini is in the form of man.' 'And afterwards, what will you create?' 'The sign of the crab (Cancer), for man, when he rises from his toil and reaps from it, will become strengthened like a lion. Then I will create the virgin (Virgo), because man will then be happy, like a virgin at her nuptials. After that I will create scales (Libra), for then, man's deeds will be measured as on scales. Afterwards I will create the scorpion (Scorpio), for when man's deeds will be weighed, it will be discovered that he also sinned, and he will have to descend to Purgatory; whereupon I will create the bow (Sagittarius), for man will surely plead for mercy and he will then be sprung from punishment, like an arrow from a bow. Then I will create the goat (Capricorn), for when man ascends, he will dart like a mountain goat. I will then create the dipper (Aquarius) to pour upon him the cleansing waters. Last, I will create fish (Pisces), to show that just as the evil eye has no effect on fish in the water, who are hidden from sight, so too Israel rises above this mundane world and neither star nor hour has absolute determination over it.'"

Rabbenu Bachaya, in his book *Kad Hakemach* (83), quotes the abovementioned Pesikta, and interprets it as referring to the process of divine reward for the performance of *mitzvot,* and retribution for the worship of false gods. He ends the passage by saying, "Open your eyes and see the lessons of the signs of the zodiac. They come to teach us that although the powers of the constellations are exceedingly great, and from the beginning of the creation their influence governs the mundane world, there is a power beyond them; the power of the Holy One, blessed be he, who chose the month of scales (Libra) to enact the day of judgment, when he decides the fate of his entire creation."

The Midrash Tanhuma (on Deuteronomy, portion Ha'azinu) associates the order of the appearance of the signs of the zodiac with the development and spiritual evolution of man, from birth to death and beyond.

The specific connotations of the various months of the year are also explained in the *Zohar.* For example, regarding the month of Sivan. whose sign is Gemini, it states, "Why was the Torah given to the Jewish people during the month whose sign is twins (Gemini)? In order that the nations of the world would not be able to claim, 'Had You given the Torah to us, we would have accepted it.' Now the Holy One, blessed be he, says, 'I gave the Torah to the Jews during the month of Gemini so that if Esau (Jacob's twin brother) would come forth and convert, and sincerely repent of his evil deeds, there will come a time when he too will study Torah.'" Jacob and Esau divided the influences of the months between them. Jacob took Nissan and Iyar (Aries and Taurus), and Esau took Tammuz and Av (Cancer and Leo); as we may observe, during those two months, due to Israel's sinfulness, the Prince of Esau (Rome) was strengthened and was able to visit retribution upon the Jewish people. As for Sivan (Gemini), these two brothers are partners to its influence, hence the sign Gemini (twins).

In the course of the book *Above the Constellations,* we attempt to explain the significance that each of the astrological signs holds for the Jewish people. This book, therefore, treads the path that *Bnei Yisaschar* and Rabbi Zaddok Hakohen followed, through the *Sefer Yetzirah.* We have also added materials derived from Ibn Ezra's book *Reshith Chochmah VeSefer HaTa'amim* (*The Beginning of Wisdom: The Book of Reasons*), which also speaks at length about the spiritual significance of the signs of the zodiac.

As with our previous books (*Mystical Glory of Shabbat and the Festivals, Glory is Now: From Hinduism Back to Judaism, Sparks is Now: Letters of Fire,* and *Happiness is Now: Revelations about Marriage*), it is the intention of this book to show the breadth of understanding and the depth of wisdom of the Jewish tradition, so that it may be compared with the cultural wisdom of the other nations.

It is our hope that, with the help of God, those who have in the past gone astray will achieve understanding and realize that within the Jewish tradition one may find a source of living water that will satisfy the seeker's search for wisdom in a way that is much more satisfying than if he were to fill his vessels from strange wells that do not hold pure water.

NISSAN
Aries (Lamb)

The month of Nissan was created through the letter Heh (ה). The ruling attribute of this month is the power of speech. It is stated in the Talmud (*Menachot,* 29b) that the letter Heh most essentially characterizes the divine act of the creation of the present world. Correspondingly, the divine act of speech was the means through which the world was created; as indicated in Tehillim (Psalms, ch. 33, v. 6), "By the word of God were the heavens made," and further (ibid, v. 9), "For He spoke and it came to be, He commanded and it was established."

The birth of the creation of this world occurred during Nissan, whereas the conception of the world occurred during Tishrei (Libra) (see *Tosaphot Rosh Hashana,* 27a).

During the month of Nissan, the expressive power of speech finds its focus in the holiday of Pesach (Passover). The holy Ari (*Pri Etz Chaim*) points out that the word "Pesach" is actually a conjugation of two words—*peh sach*—the mouth speaks. This evidently refers to the main highlight of Passover night—the recital of the Haggadah, the story of our Exodus from Egypt.

Fire is the ruling element of this month. The association of this powerful element with Nissan concurs with its being designated the official beginning of the year as regards the coronation of kings (and the dating of financial documents).

According to the holy Ari, within the structure of the cosmic body, the month of Nissan corresponds to the head, the resting place of the brain, which controls the body as a king controls his kingdom. The designation of the head is also symbolic of the fact that Nissan is the first month of the year.

The element fire reaches expression in the sacrifice of the paschal lamb. The fire roasts the lamb—the symbol of Aries, the god of the ancient Egyptians.

The science of astrology tells us that a person born under the sign of Aries excels in the tendency toward leadership. The negative expression of this principle, however, shows itself in feelings of excessive self-importance and tyranny. These qualities were most characteristic of the ancient Egyptian kingdom that enslaved the Jewish people. Therefore, the intentions behind the laws and customs of Passover are to symbolically reverse these negative tendencies.

The month of Nissan marks the beginning of the formation of the Jewish nation. This process started on the eve of our Exodus from Egypt and culminated during the third month (Sivan—Gemini) with our receiving the Torah at Mount Sinai.

According to the Avnei Nezer, this nation-building process is symbolized in the procession of the first three astrological signs: Aries, the lamb, symbolizes the unity of the collective, for in a flock of lambs, each feels that it is identical to the others. Also, just as sheep follow the shepherd, the Jewish people accepted the authority of Moses. In addition, the paschal sacrifice serves as a ritual of unification for the Jewish people.

The second month, Iyar (Taurus), symbolizes individuality, just as the bull, the astrological symbol of the month, desires to live in isolation. Iyar is therefore designated as a time of introspection and self-development in preparation for receiving the Torah.

The Shem MiShmuel states that the process of individualization associated with the month of Iyar is linked to the counting of the Omer, most of which occurs during that month. Looking at our history, it has been noted that the death of the students of Rabbi Akiva, which occurred during the Omer-counting period, was brought about by the overemphasis of the individual as opposed to the collective, which led to the neglect of the qualities of leadership and trust.

During the month of Nissan, the Jewish people expressed themselves collectively by assuming the nature of sheep following a shepherd. During the month of Iyar, however, there were times when the Jewish people expressed the rebellious qualities of the bull. When in the Sinai Desert, they rebelled against Moses and Aaron during that month.

The Pesikta Rabbah explains that the Torah wasn't given to the Jewish people during the first two months (Nissan and Iyar) because both months are symbolized by animals, whereas Sivan, when the Torah was given, is symbolized in the human form (twins).

The *Bnei Yissachar* (Discourse on Sivan) states that during the first two months, the Jewish people worked to develop their animal qualities in the service of man, and during the third month they achieved a holy human stature.

The Torah calls Nissan "Chodesh Ha'Aviv," the month of spring. Here, too, we find the symbol of development and maturation. This can also be observed in the procession of the letters that form the word *aviv* (spring): Aleph, Beth, Yod, Beth. The word begins with the unfolding of the "aleph-beth" in its ascending order. By contrast, Tishrei (תשרי)—with its letters Tav (ת), the last letter of the aleph-beth, Shin (ש), next to the last, Resh (ר), the third to the last, all in retrograde pattern returning to the Yod (י)—symbolizes a reversal of the pattern of growth that characterizes Nissan.

These tendencies are codified in the seasons of the year. Nissan, the beginning of spring, is a period of growth and agricultural development; Tishrei, marking the onset of winter, is the period when the trees lose their leaves and crops are harvested.

The process of development and unfolding is further symbolized by the combination of letters that form the divine Name, as it is associated with this month: Yod, Heh, Vav, Heh. The Yod symbolizes wisdom, which in the unfolding of the process of creation precedes the Heh, which symbolizes understanding. They give birth to the Vav, the six attributes (grace, judgment, beauty, victory, glory, and foundation) that are unified in the last Heh, kingdom, which corresponds to the world of action.

Kingdom, symbolized by the last Heh, denotes growth and agriculture, which proceed through the attribute of abundant grace. This attribute was expressed toward the Jewish people during Nissan, when God liberated them from Egyptian bondage although the Jews of that time did not merit it. The Jews at that time expressed grace by their powerful faith and purity, as it is written (Jeremiah, ch. 2, v. 2), "I remember you for the affection of your youth and the espousal of your love; how you followed Me in the wilderness in a land that was not sown." So, too, the attribute of grace is expressed in the creation of the world, which, as mentioned earlier, has its roots in this month; as it is written (Psalms, ch. 89, v. 3), "For I have said, the world is built on grace (and kindness)."

The attribute of grace is further indicated in the combination, appropriate for this month, of the letters of the divine Name. When we spell out the unfolding of this name—Yod; Yod, Heh; Yod, Heh, Vav; Yod, Heh, Vav, Heh—its numerical value is 72, the same as the numerical value of *chesed,* grace. This implies that grace in both this world and the world above are expressed during this month.

The wisdom of astrology tells us that one born during this month has a natural tendency to kindness and generosity. This tendency on the part of the Jewish people attains its fruition in their observance of the Torah and its commandments.

The heavenly body that rules Aries is Mars, which symbolizes the power of (stern) judgment. The relationship between grace and judgment was clearly expressed in the liberation of the Jewish people from Egypt, which resulted in grace toward the liberated and retribution against their oppressors. So, too, in our awaited future liberation, during the month of Nissan—the month of liberation—retribution will be meted out to the oppressors of Israel, and grace will be expressed toward Israel.

The working together of the principles of grace and judgment can also be seen in the Passover sacrifice, in which the lamb, symbolizing grace, is roasted on the fire, symbolizing judgment. An essential aspect of the Passover rituals is the harmonization of grace and judgment.

The nations most affected by the sign of Aries are Israel and the Arab countries. In fact, Aries, being the first-born—so to speak—of the astrological constellations, was the sign of ancient Egypt, the most powerful nation of that time. At the height of their constellation's influence, at the fifteenth day of the lunar month, when Egypt was deriving the most power from its ruling star, the Jewish people were delivered from them. This expresses the fact that all of nature is under divine rule (see *Bnei Yisaschar,* Discourse on Nissan).

As mentioned earlier, the sign of Aries, in its negative aspect, expresses itself as false pride and dictatorship. These qualities were characteristic of Pharaoh and the Egyptians, who believed only in themselves and denied divine guidance. Their illusions were shattered.

During Passover we refrain from eating any food that contains leavening—which symbolizes pride, for it causes dough to rise and puff up. We also eat matzoh, which symbolizes humbleness—bread that doesn't rise. False pride can lead a person to an unrealistically high self-estimation, and to brashness of ego. It is to counteract these influences that the Torah and its commandments were given.

The sheep (Aries) at the head of its herd does not consider itself to be the most important one, for it recognizes, along with the others, the guidance of the shepherd. So, too, the central concept of Passover is the recognition of faith in divine guidance, which counteracts the negative influences of the sign of Aries.

Of the twelve tribes of Israel, the tribe associated with this month is Judah, the tribe of King David. Kingdom is the foundation of this month, as can be derived from the verse (Exodus, ch. 12, v. 2), "This month (Nissan) shall be for you (*lachem*) the head of all months. It shall be the first month of the year for you (*lachem*)." The word *lachem*, with its letters (לכם) rearranged, spells *melech* (מלך)—king.

It is explained in the holy Kabbalah that the source of the power of kingdom rests with humbleness. This concept is also indicated in (King) David's name: Daleth, Vav, Daleth (or, Daleth V'Daleth)—humbleness and humbleness. So, too, it appears in the name Judah, where we find the letter Daleth (humbleness) placed in the middle of the divine Name: Yod, Heh, Vav, Daleth, Heh. The divine Name itself also expresses humbleness, as can be seen in the numerical values of its letters when fully spelled out: Yod (Yod, 10; Vav, 6; Daleth, 4 = 20), Heh (Heh, 5; Aleph, 1 = 6), Vav (Vav, 6; Vav, 6 = 12). Of all the letters of the aleph-beth, these letters contain the lowest numerical value when the letters are fully spelled out.

The sheep at the head of its flock may be taken as a symbol of the king at the head of his dominion. The sheep, as it walks, bleats out "Meh"—which, translated into Hebrew, means, "What are we?" Here, too, we see the combination of royalty and humbleness.

Like the lamb at the head of its flock, the tribe of Judah was always the first tribe to start traveling during the Israelites' wanderings in the desert. The rest of the tribes then followed in the formation of their correspondence to the signs of the zodiac (see the Ari, *Shaar HaPesukim*).

The name Judah symbolizes prayer, thankfulness, and acknowledgment of the truth that comes from others. Upon the birth of Judah, our Matriarch Leah exclaimed, "This time I shall praise (*odeh*) God." The development of the power of prayer reached its climax in the prayers and psalms of King David.

In Kabbalah, we find the power of speech associated with the attribute of kingdom—the word that guides and rules. This may be seen in the usage of the Hebrew word for speech, *daber*, in the following verse (Psalms, ch. 47, v. 4), "He subdued (yadber) peoples under us and nations under our feet."

Speech proceeds from the attribute of judgment and is associated with Mars, which rules the constellation of Aries. The relationship between kingdom and speech is expressed by the letter Heh, which symbolizes them both; Heh is the letter of the month whose power is speech, which proceeds from the last Heh of the divine Name whose attribute is kingdom. The sound of the letter Heh is a breath, which must always precede speech.

In another account of the relationship between the cosmic body with the months of the year, Nissan is symbolized by the heart that flows with kindness and generosity. In this structure, Tishrei corresponds to the head, whereas, according to the previous figuring that placed Nissan at the head, Tishrei corresponds to the heart. In either case, just as both Nissan and Tishrei are designated as the first month of the year—each within its own context—so, too, both the head and the heart can be said to share rulership of the body, each expressing itself in accordance with its essence. Accordingly, the Ari designates the heart and the head for both Nissan and Tishrei.

The Midrash Tadsheh (quoted in Rabbenu Bachaya's commentary at the beginning of Exodus) states that Levi, the son of Jacob and the ancestor of Moses and Aaron, was born on the sixteenth of Nissan, the month that later was to become the time of our liberation from Egypt.

The culmination of our Exodus occurred at the splitting of the Sea of Reeds. Nachshon the son of Aminadov, of the tribe of Judah (the tribe of kings), entered the water first in an act of faith that was followed by the actual splitting of the sea. Then the rest of the Jewish people, each man with his tribe, crossed the sea.

According to the *Sefer Yetzirah* (ch. 5, Mishnah 7), the limb of the body associated with the month of Nissan is the right leg. This symbolizes the taking of the first step in the development of the Jewish nation.

IYAR
Taurus (Bull)

The month of Iyar, whose sign is Taurus, was formed by means of the letter Vav. Its essential attribute is thought. The organ in the (symbolic cosmic) body that corresponds to it is the right kidney. The tribe of Yissachar, which toils in the study of Torah, is its tribe.

Scripture (1 Kings, ch. 6, v. 3) calls Iyar the month of *ziv* (brightness) because of the increased power of the sun that makes itself evident during this month (which corresponds approximately to the solar month of May). Similarly, the Babylonian name for Iyar is etymologically related to the word *ohr* (light).

According to the *Zohar*, the Vav—the letter of this month—symbolizes truth. In relating the Vav to this month's essential attribute (thought), Rabbi Zaddok Hakohen (in *Pri Tzadik*, Bamidbar, Rosh Chodesh Iyar) explains that through one's dedication to truth, one achieves deliverance from evil thoughts.

Each day of this month participates in the mitzvah of counting the Omer. In the spiritual work involved in the counting of the Omer—a time of preparation for the receiving of the Torah on Shavuot, the fiftieth day (of the Omer)—the central motif of this ritual is the renewal of one's dedication to truthfulness and to the purification of one's thoughts. This theme is mentioned in the prayer we say upon counting the Omer:

"That we may be cleansed from the husks that obscure our essence and be purified from our uncleanliness."

This month's organ is the right kidney. The Talmud, in explaining the expression "the kidneys advise," states that the kidneys are the source of our spontaneous thoughts. The right kidney, it is said, advises constructive thought; the left, evil thought.

The source of thought lies in the secret recesses of one's personality. This secret domain is the portion inherited by the tribe of Yissachar, which has "the knowledge and the understanding of the times" (1 Chronicles, ch. 12, v. 32). This tribe's main concern was to apply its knowledge of the times to reconcile the lunar and solar calendars and to establish the beginning of each lunar month. (Note: The eleven-day difference between the lunar and solar years necessitates the adding of an extra month in the lunar year every few years, so that the lunar months retain their correspondence to the seasons, and so that Passover, which occurs during the month of Nissan—also called the month of spring—would indeed always occur at the beginning of spring.)

The ability to use secret knowledge to determine the times when the holidays and festivals would occur requires great and holy intuition so that the knowledge is applied correctly. This aptitude was developed in the people of Yissachar as a result of their God-fearing nature, in consonance with the verse (Psalms, ch. 25, v. 4), "The secrets of God are imparted to those who fear him."

The service of God through fear and awe is the prescribed form of this month (*yira,* or awe, has the same letters as Iyar). This is because the development of the fear of Heaven is a prerequisite for receiving the Torah, as it is written, "The fear of Heaven is the beginning of wisdom."

The attribute of fear is related to the attribute of power. This is indicated by the equality of the numerical value of the two words: *gevurah* (power) and *yira* (fear). Power is the most outstanding attribute of the bull, the sign of this month. The sign of the bull is placed after the sign of the lamb (Aries), which symbolizes love and kindness, the qualities that express the nature of Nissan. Upon achieving one's completeness in the realm of love and kindness, one balances these "giving" attributes with power, awe, and restraint. In this way, one attains a wholeness of consciousness that enables one to both love and fear God, so that one has a firm foundation for keeping the Torah and its commandments.

Many traditional Jewish works on astrology regard the period of Iyar as being especially auspicious for healing (see *Bnei Yisaschar,* Discourse on Iyar). This is encoded in the word Iyar, whose letters from the acronym aleph—ani, Yod—Hashem, Resh—*rofecha:* "I am God your healer" (Exodus, ch. 15, v. 6). The word Iyar also has the same numerical value as the word *aruch* (remedy).

The *Bnei Yisaschar* (ibid.) offers the following explanation for the abovementioned connection: The primary causes of illness are due to either the eating of improper foods, or improper digestion and assimilation. Because during Iyar (on the fifteenth day, the full moon) the Jewish people who wandered the desert with Moses began eating the manna, the "food of angels," which contains no waste and is totally assimilated by the body, this month received the positive healing influence within it.

The miraculous traveling well of Miriam also appeared for the Jewish people in the desert during this month.

Sincere thought and deep reflection are most important for the development of one's spiritual path. These spiritual drives were nourished by the eating of the manna, which brought lucidity to the mind; the drinking from the well of Miriam purified the heart so that it was attuned to the light of truth.

As Iyar marked the commencement of the appearance of the manna and the well, it became a time, in the course of the history of the Jews, of new beginnings. The first census-taking of the Jewish people in the desert began on the first of Iyar (Numbers, ch. 1, v. 1). King Solomon began building the holy Temple on the first of Iyar (1 Kings, ch. 6, v. 1). When the Jews returned from the Babylonian exile, they began work on the construction of the second holy Temple on the first of Iyar (Ezra, ch. 3, v. 6).

The heavenly body that rules Taurus (Iyar) is Venus. This planet is associated with the qualities of deep feeling and sentiment. This planet is the causative agent for this month's being assigned the attribute of thought as its guiding principle, and the right kidney as its chief advisor.

Within the Hebrew word for Venus (*Nogah*) we find a symbol for the realm of the mysterious. This is done by adding the value of the letter to each of its letters, so that Nun becomes Samech, Gimel becomes Daleth, and Heh becomes Vav. In this way, *Nogah* turns into the word *sod* (secret).

The power of the realm of the mysterious reaches its climax on the thirty-third day of the Omer, on the eighteenth (in numbers, referred to as *chai,* or life) of Iyar, when the great spokesman of the *Zohar* (the quintessential work of Kabbalah, the Jewish mystical tradition), Rabbi Shimon bar Yochai, passed on to the next world. Just prior to his passing, he gathered his greatest students around his deathbed and revealed to them the deepest secrets of creation (see *Zohar,* vol. III, 287b *ff.*).

The power of the mystery and its understanding, as it was revealed to the tribe of Yissachar, is related to the letter Vav, the letter that formed the month of Iyar. The Vav symbolizes the divine attribute of *yesod* (foundation). The Yod in *yesod* symbolizes wisdom, which contains all attributes in potential, and *sod* denotes the secret of its unfolding. The place of this mystery is in the attribute of Iyar, thought.

The numerical value of Vav—6—symbolizes the six divisions of the Mishnah, the foundation of the Oral Torah. According to the *Bnei Yisaschar,* the beginning of the revelation of the Oral Torah occurred during the month of Iyar, when those who were unable to bring the paschal sacrifice during Nissan (through no fault of their own) appealed to Moses for a second chance. This was granted to them on the fourteenth day of Iyar. This "second Passover" resulted from the verbal interaction between people dedicated to the service of God, and thus became the source of the development of the Oral tradition.

The rectification of thought—that is, the focal point of our introspective service to God during the month of Iyar—follows directly upon the spiritual work engaged in during Nissan, the development of the awareness and control in the realm of speech. After purifying the most direct expression of the heart, the act of speech, one is enabled to refine oneself on the more subtle plane of thought and, through purifying them both (speech and thought), to become a fitting vessel for the main event in the month that follows (Sivan—Gemini): the receiving of the Torah.

The planet Venus imparts, as its influence, beauty and gracefulness. These energies are engaged in the divine service for this month, the refining of the Vav, the letter of the month, which contains six attributes—grace, power, beauty, victory, everlastingness, glory (unbiased acceptance), and foundation—which proceed from the heart. It is the harmonization of these six attributes that is the ultimate purpose of the counting of the Omer. To aid this endeavor, it has become customary during this period to study the Tractate *Ethics of the Fathers,* which contains six chapters.

The letter Vav of the divine Name (Yod, Heh, Vav, Heh) is associated with the six attributes that arise from the union of thought and understanding. The attributes are further refined through fear of God and by the development of the conscious control of one's inclinations.

The energy for this work is contained in the sign of this month, the bull, which symbolizes the power of judgment. Regarding the bull, the prophet Isaiah says (Isaiah, ch. 1, v. 3), "The bull knoweth its master, the mule the stall of its master." The bull thus symbolizes perceptive discriminatory knowledge, as is also indicated by the Hebrew synonym for bull (the word usually used is *shor*), *bakar,* which, according to the Shem MiShmuel, is etymologically related to the Hebrew word *bikur,* discernment and investigation. The word *shor* is also related to the word *shur* (gazing). Herein lies the connection between understanding, judgment, and power.

Astrology tells us that the element of Taurus is earth. Arriving as it does after the element of fire (Nissan—Aries), it instructs us further as to the nature of the spiritual work required of us during Iyar, self-collection and focus, so that our tendencies become objectively tangible to us just as the earth is tangible to us and can be manipulated by us. This is available to us after we have received the energy of fire of Nissan, which imparts grace (and power). The culmination of the service of Iyar, the month of *ziv* (brightness), occurs during the month of Sivan. The words are phonetically related to each other, for they possess the Yod, Vav in common: Sivan, *ziv,* and both the Samech (of Sivan) and the Zayin (of *ziv*) share in their being letters formed by the combination of tongue and teeth. The Nun of Sivan, containing the numerical value of 50, symbolizes the power of purity. Thus, the power of brightness of Iyar comes to fullness during the month of Sivan on the festival of Shavuot, which occurs fifty days after Passover. Between Passover, which occurs during Nissan, and Shavuot, which occurs during Sivan, is the month of Iyar, which functions as the link between the two. This is also symbolized by the letter Vav, which in Hebrew has the morphological quality of linking. (The Vav, used as a prefix, means "and.")

The letter Vav, which has the form of a straight line (shorter than the Nun), and has the numerical value of 6, symbolizes the neck, which contains six linked bones. Astrology tells us that the neck is the part of the body corresponding to the sign of Taurus.

The symbolic energy of Iyar, thought, became manifest in a negative form in the realm of desire during this month, when the Jews of the desert complained to Moses about not having meat to eat (see commentary of the Gaon of Vilna on *Sefer Yetzirah,* par. 46). The retribution of Heaven visited upon them proceeded from the attribute of judgment, operative during Iyar, through its sign, the bull.

During this month, in the Sinai Desert, the Jewish people manifested a strong desire for comfort and relaxation. These desires emanated from earth, the element of the month, which is the least energetically vibrant of the elements. The rebellion of the Jews also reflected the stubborn and rebellious nature of the bull.

Nissan and Iyar mark the approach of the summer months. In the year's seasonal cycle, they stand in opposite correspondence to Tishrei and Cheshvan (Libra and Scorpio), which signal the approach of winter. Tishrei and Cheshvan are characterized by the tribes of the two sons of Joseph, Menashe and Ephraim. The symbolic expression associated with Cheshvan is the sense of smell. According to the Ra'avad (commentary on *Sefer Yetzirah*), when Joseph withstood the seductive efforts of Potiphar's wife (see Genesis, ch. 39), his "sense of smell"—his sense of intuitive discernment—extended to all matters in the earth's domain.

According to Rabbi Zaddok Hakohen (*Discourse on Cheshvan,* commentary on Genesis), the relationship between Joseph and the sense of smell expresses itself in the equation of the sense of smell with purity of intention and thought, and the fear of Heaven. He offers, as evidence for this, the passage in Isaiah (ch. 2, v. 3), "And the delightfulness of his odor shall be due to his fear of God." The passage talks of the future Messiah. The verse continues, "He shall judge the people, but not from evidence derived from sight or hearing." The Talmud asks, "How then will he judge? By the pure intuition of his sense of smell." The sense of smell is therefore associated with wholeness (as in the Messiah), holiness, purity, and discernment. When the sense of smell is fully developed, these other characteristics are also fully manifest.

The flood that destroyed all of creation, except for Noah and his family and those animals he saved, occurred during the month of Cheshvan, the month of Menashe, Joseph's firstborn. The flood came about as a punishment for the excessive lewdness and dishonesty of Noah's generation. These expressions damaged the attribute of *yesod,* the foundation (which, in the cosmic symbolic body, corresponds to the phallus), the letter Vav. The sin of that generation expressed the very opposite of Joseph's nature as he withstood the test of Potiphar's wife.

Rabbi Zaddok Hakohen explains that the main form that service to the Divine takes during Cheshvan is the perfection of the fear of God and the acceptance of the "yoke of Heaven." Coming as it does after the month of Tishrei, which is full of festivals, culminating in the festival of Simchat Torah (The Joy of the Torah), the month of Cheshvan is set aside for the integration of the sacred joy one experiences during Tishrei.

As Nissan, with its festival Passover, corresponds to Tishrei (six months later), Iyar corresponds to Cheshvan. We may therefore expect to find many examples of correspondence.

The letter Vav of Iyar symbolizes Joseph, the sixth of the seven "shepherds" of the Jewish people (Abraham, Isaac, Jacob, Moses, Aaron, Joseph, and David), who correspond to the seven attributes of grace, power, beauty, victory, glory, foundation, and kingdom. The Vav also denotes *yesod* (foundation), the sixth of the "lower" divine attributes, which also symbolizes Joseph. So, too, the attribute of Iyar, thought, has a definite causal link to the effect of the symbolic metaphysical manifestation of *yesod,* the phallus. Also, Joseph, which in Hebrew is etymologically related to the concept of addition and joining (as is clear from the verse spoken by his mother, the Matriarch Rachel, upon giving birth to him: "Yoseph Hashem li ben aher"—"May Hashem join me in an additional son"), is symbolized by the Vav, which is morphologically related to the concept of addition and means "hook," an implement that joins two things together (see *Zohar,* vol. 1, 182b, and *Pri Tzadik,* Iyar). The bull, the sign of Taurus, Iyar, is used to symbolize Joseph in the following verse (Deuteronomy, ch. 33, v. 7), "His firstborn bullock, majesty is his, and his horns are the horns of a wild bull."

Just as the month of Cheshvan serves to unify the heart with the experiences of the festival month of Tishrei, the month of Iyar, with its attribute of thoughtful introspection, serves to internalize the holy wisdom of Passover. These sequences occur in order to bring about a strengthening and consolidation of one's awareness of the fear of God, and mastery over one's natural inclinations.

Correspondence is also evident in the astrological symbols of these months, the bull (Taurus—Iyar) and the scorpion (Scorpio—Cheshvan). Both animals are known for their self-willed stubbornness. The Torah, with its mitzvot, works to modify these traits and to attach them to the service of God. The negative expression of these traits may easily lead to man's self-destruction.

The path toward self-development through Torah and mitzvot is illustrated in the order of appearance of the forms of the astrological signs (see Shem MiShmuel, *Discourse on Iyar*). The shepherd does not demand any labor of his sheep; on the contrary, his main concern is finding them nourishing pasture. So, too, during Nissan, the heavenly interaction with the Jewish people takes the form of unconditional love, grace, and caring. This is the spirit in which Passover is celebrated; we experience and reciprocate these feelings. After we have built a strong foundation of love of God during the month of Nissan (which corresponds to the tribe of Judah, the tribe that brings glory to God by manifesting royalty and thereby unifying the Jewish people as one heart), one begins to complement the state of grace with the attributes of restraint and awe. This is achieved through mindfulness (symbolized by thought) concentrated on the service of God through Torah. From a lamb one becomes like a bull carrying the burden of Torah. One contracts the expansiveness of love and reveals the awesome majesty of God through the conscientious search for, and the making of oneself into a vessel worthy to receive, truth. The letter Vav that formed the month of Iyar is a symbol for truth; just as the Vav is a morphological connector, the truth can always be verified by the facts that it is connected to.

In the hierarchy of values of the heart, faith, symbolized by Nissan, precedes truth, symbolized by Iyar. Nissan's service is communal, whereas Iyar's service is individual.

The *Zohar* has a different system of assigning the correspondences of the tribes to the months than the system of the Ari, which we have been following up to now. The Ari bases his correspondences in the travel and encampment formation of the Jewish people in the desert, as they are described in the beginning of Numbers. The *Zohar,* however, bases its correspondences on the order of birth of the twelve sons of Jacob, as described in Genesis.

According to the *Zohar,* Nissan corresponds to Reuben, Iyar to Simon, and Sivan to Levi. The Shem MiShmuel (ibid.) examines these correspondences and tries to shed light on the teachings they may yield for the divine service. Nissan corresponds to seeing, for *reiyah* (vision) is the root word of the name Reuben, as our Matriarch Leah remarked when she named him (Genesis, ch. 29, v. 32): "Ra'ah Hashem beonyi"—"God has been my affliction." Iyar, corresponding to Simon, denotes the faculty of hearing, as Leah stated upon naming him: "Shamah Hashem"—"God has surely heard . . ." (ibid., v. 33).

The sight and divine awareness of Nissan is aroused from Above (just as—usually—sight is associated with some external object in the field of vision), and brings a person to realize the divine Providence. This was clearly revealed to us in the great vision of the grace of God that the Jewish people experienced at the crossing of the Sea of Reeds; as it is written (Exodus, ch. 14, vol. 31), "And Israel saw the great Hand. . . ." So, too, in all future generations, a person may merit the grace of God by his divine service, in realizing that it is due only to one's God-given strength and inspiration that one can engage in such divine service.

During the month of Iyar, the divine Light is not as close to us, but is appreciated from afar, as it were, just as hearing is from afar. The full appreciation of what is heard can only be achieved by a person in full conscious awareness. Only then can one gather the full depth and nuances of the meaning of what is heard. So, too, during Iyar, it is demanded that one deepen his understanding of the ways of God even though at the time he may not be directly perceiving the "hand of God."

The element of fire and the light that emanates from it, which is a characteristic of Nissan, is given to one in preparation for the work of self-understanding in times of darkness, when one is under the influence of the earth element of Iyar.

The combined service of Nissan and Iyar brings one to the month of Sivan (Gemini—twins), the month of Levi. The name Levi is etymologically related to the word *leveyah* (joining), as we may gather from the remark of our Matriarch Leah upon naming him: "Ata yelave ishi"—"Now my man shall be joined unto me." During Sivan, the month of the holiday of Shavuot, when we receive the Torah, we attain the grace of being joined with and bound to God, the Holy One, blessed be he.

SIVAN
Gemini (Twins)

The sign of Sivan is Gemini. Its letter is Zayin; according to the Ari, its tribe is Zevulun. The attribute of this month is travel. Travel symbolizes the practical result of the sacred development of the power of speech that characterizes Nissan, and the attribute of thought that characterizes Iyar, as it is written, "In your wanderings and travelings, this (Torah) shall be your subject of conversation." During these three months we attempt to perfect ourselves in the realms of thought, speech, and action, which together constitute the whole expression of man and the complete fulfillment of the Torah and its commandments.

That travel (the attribute of this month) symbolizes the realm of action is further indicated in the letter that formed this month, the Zayin, which has a numerical value of seven and symbolizes the material plane, which is built on the sevenfold principle, as seen in the seven days of the week, the seven colors of the spectrum, and the seven tones of the musical scale. The seventh of the divine attributes, kingdom, symbolizes the realm of action.

As a word, the letter Zayin denotes tools, as in implements of the material technologies of agriculture or war, for the word Zayin can mean weaponry or may be seen as etymologically related to the word *mazon* (foodstuff).

For the month of Sivan, this symbol denotes the giving of the Torah, the weapon against one's evil inclination, and the source of spiritual sustenance. On the material plane, we notice that Sivan is the month when (in Israel) wheat is harvested.

The relationship between Torah, weaponry, and food is expressed in the passage (Proverbs, ch. 25, v. 21), "If your enemy be hungry, feed him bread." Our sages say that bread may be understood here as a symbol for the wisdom of the Torah, or spiritual sustenance; the Hebrew word for bread, *lechem,* is etymologically related to the word for war, *milchama.* In the spiritual realm, this refers to the war that one must conduct against one's baser instincts. Thus, if one's enemy—i.e., one's baser inclinations—are in need of sustenance, feed them in a way associated with Torah.

Both travel (Sivan's attribute) and food (implied in this month's letter) are indicated in the function of the tribe of Zevulun (the tribe associated with this month), which would engage in commerce and foreign trade and thereby would fulfill its part in the spiritual partnership between them and the tribe of Yissachar. Yissachar studies, and Zevulun provides that tribe with all its physical needs; together, they share in the maintenance of the Torah and in its rewards. This partnership is symbolized by the sign of this month, Gemini (twins).

The element of Sivan is air. Just as air is essential for life to continue, so, too, the teachings of the Torah are essential for the maintenance of the world.

The holy *Zohar* says, "Because Jacob is a twin to Esau, the Torah was given during the sign of Gemini." (See *Pri Tzadik,* vol. 4, Rosh Chodesh Sivan—Bamidbar.) The twinship of Jacob and Esau calls attention to the story of Jacob receiving the blessings of the firstborn. Through this, Jacob enabled both himself and his brother Esau to achieve wholeness in the service of God.

Following the idea that the twins of Gemini represent Jacob and Esau, Rabbi Zaddok Hakohen (ibid.) explains that the first three months of the year are symbolized by the three

Patriarchs. Nissan is symbolized by Abraham, denoting the attributes of grace and kindness; Iyar is symbolized by Isaac, denoting judgment and power; and Jacob symbolizes Sivan, denoting beauty and meditation. The Talmud (*Berachot,* 58a) states that in the verse of King David's blessing (1 Chronicles, ch. 29, v. 11), which is also the scriptural source of the seven attributes discussed in Kabbalah, "Thine, o Lord, is the greatness, the power, the beauty." "The beauty" refers to the giving of the Torah, for the Torah mediates and unifies greatness (the revelation of grace) and (judgment) power.

The heavenly body that influences the month of Sivan is Mercury. This planet is associated with communication and intelligence. These qualities find concurrence in the events of Jewish history that happened during this month. During this month, we received the Torah. This gave us the vehicle with which to unify our consciousness and the means of direct communication with the Divine; thus, it provides us with an enduring way of life. The speed of Mercury is denoted in the letter assigned to it by the *Sefer Yetzirah,* the Resh, which by its sound is intuitively associated with speed.

In the science of astrology we find that each sign contains its own characteristics. We also find that the twelve signs are divided into four groups, each containing three signs. Each group follows a certain pattern, consisting of the structural order of function, stabilization, and change. Thus, each group shares similar characteristics with the others. Accordingly, Nissan, Tammuz, Tishrei, and Tevet correspond to function; Iyar, Av, Cheshvan, and Shevat correspond to stabilization; and Sivan, Elul, Kislev, and Adar correspond to change. Each of these changing months (of which Sivan is the first) brought about, in the course of Jewish history, some new dimension that caused a forward movement and development. Sivan contributed the giving of the Torah; Elul, the element of *teshuvah,* return to God and rectification of past deeds; Kislev, the holiday of Chanukah and the flowering of the Oral tradition; and Adar, Purim, the unification of the Jewish people in exile.

The knowledge of this process of development (function, stabilization, and change) is useful in one's inner work and may also serve to guide one through these months. The service to the Divine during Nissan, expressed in kindness and in holiness of speech, demands that its function be expressed in positive action. Typically, this occurs during the holiday of Passover by expressing one's magnanimity toward the poor; the invitation of guests; and the special Passover talk centered around the Haggadah.

Iyar, the month of stabilization, demands an inner rectification of thought, and makes use of one's sense of judgment and discernment. Thereby it brings one into a clearer focus and stabilization so that one is not swayed by incidental feelings.

After we set right the energies of heart and mind (Nissan and Iyar), we are ready for Sivan and the process of movement and travel, so that the results of the change may be beneficial.

The full effects of positive change were felt by the Jewish people during this month. At the beginning of the month, the Jewish people reached the Sinai Desert (in Hebrew, *Midbar Sin*). The name Sivan contains the letters of the name *sin* (Samech, Yod, Nun) with the connecting letter Vav. The process of change came to expression in the feeling of internal unity of the entire Jewish nation, which occurred in an unprecedented manner and has not been experienced in such totality since then. The Torah described this when it said (Exodus, ch. 19, v. 2), "Vayichan sham Yisrael"—"And Israel rested facing the mountain." The grammatical form used for the word "rested" is the singular rather than the plural form (*vayichan,* not *vayachanu*). This is the only time that the singular form is used in describing Israel's encampments during their wanderings. The commentator Rashi explains the significance of this as follows: "They (the Jewish people) rested as one man with one heart." The unification of various types of people is denoted in the sign of the month, twins.

Astrology lists as characteristics of Gemini flexibility and instability, complexity, non-rootedness, and moodiness. Because Israel rises above the influence of the constellations, these traits can be modified by the observance of the Torah. The non-fixation that gives rise to instability turns to attainment of flexibility of consciousness after being freed from the fixation of being slaves in Egypt.

Mercury, which influences Gemini (Sivan) and also Virgo (Elul), is set aside for repentance and return to God. This must imply a personal non-fixation. Furthermore, both Sivan and Elul are symbolized by the human form. This human symbolism points to these months as being auspicious for the development of one's spiritual inclinations.

According to the Ari, the twelve months of the year derive from the letter Vav of the divine Name (Yod, Heh, Vav, Heh). The complete spelling of the Vav—Vav, Vav—has the numerical value of 12. The first Vav corresponds to the spring and summer months; the second Vav corresponds to the fall and winter months. Being that each set of six months is symbolized by the letter Vav, each month of one set of six has a corresponding month in the other set of six. Thus, the winter months serve to complement and make whole the summer months.

The winter month that corresponds to Sivan (when the written Torah was given) is the month of Kislev, when the Hashmonaim (Maccabees) were victorious over the Syrian imperial Hellenist influence. From the period of the Maccabees and onwards, we find the beginning of the fuller development of the Oral Torah (see *Magen Avraham,* Miketz). As mentioned earlier, both of these months correspond to the "changing" months in the process of function, stability, and change.

The *Zohar* connects the tribe of Levi to the month of Sivan. Moses and Aaron, who together prepared the people of Israel to receive the Torah, were both descended from the tribe of Levi.

The tribe of Levi is divided into Kohanim (priests), the descendants of Aaron, and Leviim (who assist the Kohanim and form the Temple choir). Together they escort (*melave,* an etymological derivative of the word Levi) the Jewish people and bring them close to their Father in heaven.

According to the Ari, the month of Sivan is associated with the tribe of Zevulun. In the name Zevulun is contained the word *zevul* (tabernacle). This calls attention to the fact that, during this month, the Jewish people merited the dwelling of the divine Presence in the Temple because of their acceptance of the Torah (see Midrash Rabbah, beginning of Teruma).

These two ways of seeing the tribal correspondences (the *Zohar,* which associates Sivan with Levi; and the Ari, who associates Sivan with Zevulun) complement each other. Just as Moses and Aaron are seen as twins in their roles of bringing the Torah to the Jewish people, Yissachar and Zevulun are seen as twins in their financial–spiritual arrangement that ensures the maintenance of the Torah by the Jewish people.

Levi is the third son of Jacob, just as Sivan is the third month of the year. Sivan, the third of the spring months, marks the year's victory over winter. Correspondingly, Kislev, the third winter month, marks the Jewish victory over the third kingdom that came to enslave them (Syria–Greece, which was preceded by Babylon–Persia and Egypt).

The double form of the astrological sign (twins) is also encountered in the month of Adar, whose sign is Pisces (fishes). They also both correspond to the "changing" sign of the astrological process. The twins of Gemini correspond to the "twin Torahs," the Oral Torah and the written Torah. The month of Sivan is the time of the acceptance of the written Torah, whereas the month of Adar (which contains the holiday Purim) marks the time of our acceptance of the Oral Torah.

According to the science of astrology, people born during either of these months are drawn to the coupled influences of introversion and extroversion. In the Jewish context, this infers a capacity for both the esoteric and exoteric understanding of the Torah. In the path of the observance of the precepts of the Torah, this refers to the unity of action with deep feeling and intention.

The limb associated with Sivan is the left leg. In contrast with the right leg, which denotes grace, the left leg denotes power, calling attention to the All-powerful who gave us the Torah.

The connection between Iyar (the month that precedes Sivan and is a time for introspection) with wisdom and insight (according to *Bnei Yisaschar,* Iyar) is contained in the combination of the letters of the divine Name associated with that month (Yod, Heh, Heh, Vav), which forms the acronym of the verse (Jeremiah, ch. 9, v. 26), "Yit'halel hamit'halel haskel viyadoa"—"May the praiseworthy be praised in that he knows and understands my ways."

The combination of the divine Name for Sivan is Yod, Vav, Heh, Heh. The first two letters, Yod and Vav, are masculine, active letters that impart their influence to the last two letters, the (passive–receptive) feminine Heh.

This symbolizes the imparting of wisdom from God to the Jewish people. Here, too, we find the concept of a couple (twins), symbolizing the marriage of God with the Jewish people.

TAMMUZ
Cancer (Crab)

The astrological sign of the month of Tammuz is Cancer (crab).
The letter that forms it is the Het. The month of Tammuz is associated with Reuben, whose attribute is sight. The combination
of the divine Name associated with it is Heh, Vav, Heh, Yod. According to the Ari, the name A-donai, when fully spelled out—
Alef, Lamed, Peh; Daleth, Lamed, Tav; Nun, Vav, Nun; Yod, Vav,
Daleth—contains twelve letters, each of which corresponds to a
particular month (Aleph to Nissan, Lamed to Iyar, Peh to Sivan,
Daleth to Tammuz, etc.). Following this, we see that the two letters for Tammuz and Av (Daleth and Lamed), when combined,
spell the word *dal*, which means poor. This indicates that these
two months are poverty-stricken, so to speak, for the Jewish
people (see *Bnei Yisaschar*, on the months Tammuz and Av).
We may note this in the historical occurrences of these months,
when many tragedies befell the Jewish people. The center of
this tragic time spans the three weeks between the seventeenth
of Tammuz (which, in our history, was the day the walls of the
First and Second Temples were breached), and the ninth of Av
(when the Temples were destroyed).

According to the *Zohar*, the first three months—Nissan,
Iyar, and Sivan—were given as an inheritance to the children
of Jacob, and the next three—Tammuz, Av, and Elul—were
of the portion of Esau. After many battles, which took great

wisdom and planning on Jacob's part, the month of Elul was successfully transferred to the lot of Jacob (see *Bnei Yisaschar*), and was set aside as a time of repentance.

Correspondingly, the winter months—Tevet, Shevat, and Adar—fell to the lot of Esau. And as it was with Elul, so with Adar (the month that contains the Purim festival); it was turned over to the Jewish people.

An allusion to the initiation of the period of strict judgment marked by the month of Tammuz is found in the letter combination of the divine Name, which in this month is spelled the opposite of its original order; in place of Yod, Heh, Vav, Heh, we have Heh, Vav, Heh, Yod. The first symbolizes kindness; the second, judgment.

According to the Shem MiShmuel (*Bamidbar,* Tammuz), the three months of Tammuz, Av, and Elul are designated for the process of ascent from below to above, and, hence, the spelling of the name from below (last) is above (first). They come after the first three months of Nissan, Iyar, and Sivan, which begin with the spelling of the name from above (first) to below (last), denoting the descent of God's effluence during those first three months.

The descent from above to below during those first three months is seen in the deliverance from Egyptian bondage (Nissan), the raining of manna from heaven (Iyar), and the giving of the Torah (Sivan). After this period we come to the three summer months, when we are given the responsibility of raising even the most mundane aspects of the world to higher spiritual significance. This work began for the Jewish nation, during Tammuz, with the sending of the spies by Moses on a forty-day mission, most of which occurred during Av, to investigate the land the Jews were about to enter. Their mission failed, and, due to the false reports they brought back, the entry into the land was delayed and the door was opened to the possibility of the destruction of the two holy Temples, which occurred during these months.

The attribute of this month, sight, was put out of the realm of holiness by the sin of the spies (see *Zohar,* beginning of

Shelach). Their deep ambition to remain princes of the desert kept them from appreciating the opportunities of the land. They blemished the realm of sight by reporting back to the Jewish people the depressing aspects of living in Canaan, describing it as "a land that devours its inhabitants" (Numbers, ch. 13, v. 32).

The letter Het, in its negative aspect, denotes sinfulness and unwholesomeness (in Hebrew the word that describes this is חטא, *chet*). On the other hand, Het may also carry within it the meaning of cleansing and purification (in Hebrew, *hituy*) (see Shem MiShmuel, ibid.). By cleansing one's own heart, one also purifies his faculty of vision and his sense of sight, and he will be able to see in everything, and at every opportunity, a way of bringing glory to the divine Being.

The sense of sight is at the root of sins in the realm of the flesh. The eye sees, so the heart lusts. Lust may be described as the heart of desire, and its feeling is commensurate with a heating of the blood. So, too, the Aramaic meaning of the word Tammuz is heat, as in the verse (Daniel, ch. 3, v. 19), "Lemaze eatuna"—"To heat the furnace." So, too, as reported in Ezekiel (Ch. 3, v. 14), during this month the women of Babylon wept for lost love.

This all indicates that the period of Tammuz is noted as a time when the extreme aspects of the world have the most attraction. It is interesting to note that the crab (Cancer) is a favorite food of people who are given over to worldly pleasures and desires. This is because it is rooted in the element water, which flows as it desires. The ruling heavenly body of Cancer is the moon, which has a great effect on the waters of the earth. The negative aspect of Cancer (in Hebrew, *sartan*) is indicated in three of its letters—S, T, N—which spell the word "Satan."

This heated nature may be transformed into spiritually beneficial energy through repentance. This transformation may be observed in the person of Reuben, son of Jacob, whose tribe corresponds to this month. The Midrash Tanhuma (Bereshith) states that Reuben was the first person in the world to return to God by repenting out of love for Him.

In the ultimate future, this month, which is present in the domain of Esau, will "repent," and, instead of being a period of mourning, will be transformed into a period of gladness and rejoicing in the domain of Jacob.

It is interesting to observe how the various opinions apply the assignment of the tribes and the month to complement one another. The *Zohar* makes the correspondence between the months and the tribes based on the homological order of the tribes' births. Therefore, Nissan and Iyar correspond to Reuben and Simon. The Ari, however, who orders the correspondences according to the formation of travel of the Jewish tribes in the desert, places Reuben and Simon in Tammuz and Av.

On a deeper level, we may observe a relationship between Nissan and Iyar on the one hand, and Tammuz and Av on the other. Both sets of two months are at the beginning of seasons: Nissan marks the beginning of spring, and Tammuz the beginning of summer. They are also in the fixed places in their astrological respective cycles (fixed, active, changing). These three aspects of the cycle also correspond to the developmental process of the formation of the Jewish people as exemplified in the three Patriarchs: Abraham, Isaac, and Jacob. Abraham symbolizes grace and kindness—the active principle. Isaac symbolizes power, contraction, and fear—the fixed principle. Jacob symbolizes mediation, beauty, and truth—the changing principle.

Reuben, who bears a relationship to sight (*reu,* see; *ben,* a son), is therefore associated with wisdom and grace, and can be placed in either Nissan or Tammuz. Simon is related to hearing, understanding, and focus, and therefore to *gevurah,* and may be placed in Iyar or Av.

The element of Tammuz is water. It shares this element with the month of Cheshvan, whose sign is Scorpio. The similarity between these two months (Tammuz and Cheshvan) is contained in the meaning of the Hebrew names of their signs. *Sartan* (Cancer) contains the word *Satan,* and *akrab* (Scorpio) contains *akar* (uprooted, destroyed) and *bet* (house). This denotes that the Flood that destroyed the world, which was full of adultery and uncontrollable evil expression, occurred during the month of Cheshvan, whose element is water. Water is also the source of desire, for just as water runs freely, so does desire. The rectification of the element of water occurs during the third month containing this element, Adar. During Purim (the fourteenth and fifteenth of Adar), the attribute of desire is sanctified by the festival of eating and drinking, done in a spirit of holiness.

The emotional energy of Tammuz, with its destructive element, is symbolized in the tribe of Reuben as it conducted itself during the desert wanderings. The tribe of Reuben revolted against the authority of Moses under the instigation of Korach. And during Av (whose tribe is Simon), which is also a bad period in Jewish history, the prince of that tribe, Zimri, precipitated a revolt against Moses.

Just as the senses of hearing and sight—as the most immediate to and impressionable on us—may cause us to act on their influence alone, so with the tribes of Reuben and Simon and the months of Tammuz and Av, there exists this danger, which actually expressed itself after the Exodus.

During the time of the generation of knowledge, i.e., the generation of the wandering in the desert, which is the root generation, so to speak, of the Jewish people, these two months received their ominous imprint on Jewish history. The sin of the Golden Calf occurred during Tammuz. About this, God said, "On the day of my choosing, I shall remember it" (Exodus, ch. 32, v. 34). On the ninth of Av, the spies that Moses sent returned with an evil report about the land of Israel. Of these two occurrences, the first (Golden Calf) was due to misconstrued sight: Satan showed to the Jewish people Moses in heaven, and they believed that Moses was dead. The second sin (the spies) occurred because of the misuse of the faculty of hearing. The sin of the Golden Calf, which was idol worship, was the cause of the destruction of the First holy Temple. Out of the sin of the spies came baseless hatred, which eventually brought about the destruction of the Second Temple.

The heavenly body that influences Tammuz is the moon, whose influence on the tides of water indicates the basis of the meaning of the element of the month, water. This connection may also be observed in the attribute sight, which emerges from the eye, whose element is water. From these connections emerges the spiritual focal point of this period of the year for deep influence and change; for the power of sight and the power of desire are both rooted in water, which is ruled by the moon, whose form is constantly changing. A greater susceptibility to sense impressions, which grows out of the impact of the sense of sight, was the chief cause of the sins of the spies and the Golden Calf.

AV
Leo (Lion)

The month of Av was formed by the letter Teth. Its nature is hearing, its sign is the lion, and its tribe is Simon. The letters Heth and Teth (which spell the word *chet,* sin, which symbolizes the period of Tammuz–Av) point to this being a time of transgression. The letters Heth and Teth are not found within the names of the Patriarch Jacob's twelve sons, an indication that their souls are pure. According to the Ari, the weakness of these two months is expressed by the two letters Daleth and Lamed (in the twelve letters spelling the Name A-donai), which form the word *dal* (poor). Also, the first letters of the two tribes Reuben and Shimon (Simon), as well as the first letters of the nature of these months, *reiah* (sight) and *shemiah* (hearing), spell the word *rash* (impoverished). On the other hand, *dal* may also mean "lifting up," as in the verse (Psalms, ch. 30, v. 2), "Aromimcha Hashem ki dilisani"—"I shall praise God for he has lifted me up," for in the future God will raise us up during these months. With the next month, Elul, comes the letter Tav. The letters Daleth, Lamed, and Tav form the word *deleth* (door), symbolizing that during Elul the door to penance is open.

The misuse of the faculty of hearing is at the root of all of the tragedies that the Jews have suffered during the month of Av. The Midrash says (Rabbah, Numbers, ch. 14, v. 1) regarding the verse, "And the children of Israel wept that night," referring to the night (of the ninth of Av) that the spies of Moses returned with the evil report concerning the land of Israel, that the unnecessary weeping that the Jews engaged in then brought about their having to weep in earnest, during that time, in the generations to come.

The tragedies of the ninth of Av, the destruction of the two holy Temples of Jerusalem by Babylon and Rome, are symbolized by the sign of the month, the lion (Leo), which mercilessly rends its victims. Also, the name of this month, Av, is an acronym of the two nations that destroyed the two holy Temples: Aleph—Edom (Rome), the nation that destroyed the Second Temple and has tormented us ever since, and Beth—Babylon, which destroyed the First Temple.

The heavenly body that rules Leo, the sun, symbolizes the power of this sign, for the nations of the world reckon their calendar according to the solar year. Also, the first day of the week, Sunday, is ruled by the sun, and, as evidenced by the name of that day and by the fact that the nations of the world established their day of rest on that day, the solar symbolism is still operative. The element of this month, fire, also points to the power of the sun.

There are two negative aspects of this month. Exemplified by the transgression of the spies is the sin of pride, which our Sages say is rooted in the element of fire; the ambition to rule at all costs is symbolized by the sign of the month, the lion, the king of beasts. These attributes influenced the sensitivities of the spies, who wanted to maintain their positions as princes of the desert, and caused them to convey their false reports about the land. This, in conjunction with the essential nature of the month, hearing, on the part of the people of Israel, who accepted the spies' reports, thereby turned this month into a time of mourning and tribulation in the course of their history.

The qualities of pride and irrational self-assurance found themselves in the character of the prince of the tribe of this month, the tribe of Simon. On the plains of Moab, just prior to the Jews' crossing the border of Israel, Zimri, prince of Simon, publicly rebelled against the authority of Moses and the Torah

AV—LEO (LION)

at the instigation of Kozbi, the daughter of the Midianite prince. Her words aroused his feelings of self-importance, and, as a result of the negative influence of his shameful behavior, he caused the death of many of his tribesmen. This was due, on their part, to the uncritical acceptance of what they heard.

The combination of the divine Name for this month is Heh, Vav, Yod, Heh, which implies the attribute of stern judgment, as found in the passage (Exodus, ch. 9, v. 3), "Hinei yad Hashem hoyah bimiknicha"—"Behold the hand of God shall be upon your cattle," referring to the plague upon the Egyptians of the disease of their cattle. The word *hoyah* also carries with it the connotation of marriage rites, as explained in the Talmud (Tractate *Kedushin,* 5a). This contrast of meaning tells us, according to Rabbi Zaddok Hakohen (*Pri Tzadik,* Bamidbar), that although the month of Av carries with it the connotation of stern judgment now, in the future this month will turn into a period of joy and gladness, of the celebration of the marriage between God and the Jewish people.

The double meaning of the month of Av reveals itself as well in the letter that gave this month its form, the letter Teth. In its negative aspect it symbolizes *teet* (lime pit)—death (see *Otyot d'Rabbi Akiva,* explanation of the meaning of the Hebrew letters according to Rabbi Akiva, letter Teth), whereas in its positive aspect it is the beginning of the word *tov* (goodness). The Talmud (*Baba Kama,* 55a) teaches that a person who sees the letter Teth in a dream may expect good fortune, for the passage (Genesis, ch. 1, v. 4) states, "And God saw the light that it was good (*tov*)."

The essential nature of this month, hearing, is associated with the letter Teth in its indication that in its positive aspect, one's proper use of the hearing faculty may lead one to good works, whereas its misuse may lead one to *tumah,* impurity and destruction. Therefore, the main form that the spiritual work of this month takes is the purification of the realm of hearing and its proper association with the understanding heart, as stated in the verse from which the form of the divine Name is derived: "Keep silent (collect yourselves) and hear"—"Hasketh ushma

Yisrael hayom" (Deuteronomy, ch. 27, v. 9). The first two letters, Heh and Vav, are in the opposite of their usual order in the
divine Name, and thereby denote the first two weeks of this
month, when the period of strongest judgment is upon us. The
last two letters, Yod and Heh, although in the essential form of
the Name they are the first two letters, still are in their proper
order, and denote the last two weeks of this month, regarded as
a time of mercy and divine compassion.

The day of bad tidings, the ninth of Av, is associated, according to Kabbalah, with the hollow of the thigh (the sciatic
nerve, the place where the angel of Esau wounded Jacob), one
of the 365 veins that correspond to the days of the year. Because
this is where the angel that wrestled with our Patriarch Jacob
wounded him, therefore (Genesis, ch. 32, v. 33), "The children
of Israel may eat the sinew of the thigh vein (of animals)." The
letters *eth,* as in "eth gid hanashe" (the sinew of the thigh vein),
are an acronym for Av Tisha, the ninth of Av, and symbolizes
the wounding of that day by the evil influences.

The ninth of Av is associated with the letter Teth, which
has the numerical value of nine. The letter Teth, according to
the Talmud (*Baba Kama,* 55a), is related to destruction and
death, as in the verse (Isaiah, ch. 14, v. 23), "Vetateyah bem-
tateh hashmad"—"And I shall sweep it with destruction." In the
course of Jewish history, on the ninth of Av many other divine
decrees of destruction besides the destruction of the two holy
Temples have been visited upon us. Most notable among them
are the signing of the decree of the Spanish Inquisition and the
subsequent exile, and the many persecutions that occurred
during World War I, which started on that day. The first trans-
ports to the gas chambers during World War II also occurred
on that day. The double spelling of the letter, as in Teth (טט),
has the numerical value of 18, and has the same value as the
word *chet* (חטא), sin, to tell us that that same power of dissua-
sion from righteousness that leads to sin also visits retribution
upon those who follow this path. In the realm of holiness, the
number eighteen has the same value as the word *chai* (חי), life,
the living source of holiness.

The Davidic Messiah, from the tribe of Judah, is to be born during the month of Av. This is indicated in the verses (Genesis, ch. 49, v. 9) of Jacob's blessings to his sons: "Judah is the lion's whelp." The lion of Judah, the royal Judah (the lion is also the sign of this month), will annull, with the coming of the Messiah, the evil decrees that visit the Jewish people.

According to Rabbi Zaddok Hakohen (ibid.), the birth of the Messiah on the ninth of Av is an occurrence that may happen in any generation.

The science of astrology associates the sign of Leo with the birth of powerful world leaders, and associates this with the element of the month, fire, and with its ruling heavenly body, the sun. With the coming of the Messiah, the sun will shine forth the more brightly, when God removes the protective layer around the sun and reveals its holy fire that will destroy the evil and heal the good.

According to the *Zohar,* the tribe of the month of Av is Yissachar, the tribe of the Torah. The Torah is associated with royalty, as indicated in the verse (Proverbs, ch. 8, v. 15, and discussed in the Talmud, p. 72b), "By Me shall the princes rule." According to the Midrash, Yissachar, son of Jacob, was born on the tenth of Av (see Rabbenu Bachaya, *Shemot*). Therefore we may say that the power of rulership by means of the Torah will be revealed through the kingdom of the Messiah, as it is written (Isaiah, ch. 11, v. 2), "And the spirit of God shall rest upon him, the spirit of wisdom and understanding, the spirit of council and might, the spirit of knowledge and fear of God."

The winter month that corresponds to Av is Shevat. The common principle that binds them is revealed on the fifteenth day of both months: both are days of rejoicing. During Av, this comes after the two weeks of mourning, corresponding to the first two letters of this month's combination of the divine Name—Heh, Vav—in inverse order. The fifteenth of Av corresponds to the beginning of the second two weeks of Av, the letters Yod and Heh (and proceed according to their natural order), which reign, making it a day of joy.

The month of Shevat was formed by the letter Tzadi (צ), which has the numerical value of 90—ten times nine (Teth), the letter of Av. The name Shevat may also be read *shevet* (rod); thus, we may uncover a connection between the punishment of Av and the rod of Shevat. The name Shevat, with its connotation of rod, is said to refer to the plagues that the Egyptians suffered in that month.

ELUL
Virgo (Virgin)

The month of Elul is formed by the letter Yod. Its essential nature is action, and its sign is the virgin. These two attributes, the Yod and the virgin, symbolize the essence of the month: return to God and renewal. The letter Yod (ʾ) forms the beginning of all letters, and its meaning in this context is an indication of the necessity of building one's living processes starting from true beginnings and roots. The letter Yod is the first letter of the divine Name (Yod, Heh, Vav, Heh), and alludes to the attribute of wisdom. The sign of this month, the virgin, refers to the necessity of a person to renew his purity during this month, so that one's virginal quality becomes clear by one's nullification of the evil deeds of the past.

The meaning of the Aramaic word Elul, searching, is derived from the Targum (the first rabbinic Aramaic translation of the Torah) on the passage (Numbers, chap. 13, v. 2), "That they may spy out the land of Canaan." It imparts to the month of Elul its meaning of being an inspirational time for self-discovery and return to God. This is also revealed in the numerical value of the word Elul, which is equivalent to that of the word *binah* (understanding), which points to the process of concentration and meditation for the sake of returning to God.

The heavenly body that imparts its influence to Elul is Mercury. This planet is associated with the intellect, the tool most useful for the spiritual work of this month. Mercury also influences the sign of Gemini (Sivan), the month when the Torah was given.

The element of the month, earth, symbolizes the realm of action, the nature of the month. It is, therefore, the combination of openness in the realm of perception and thought with their proper association in the realm of action that is demanded in the work of this month. For this reason, on the first Sabbath of this month we read publicly Shoftim, the portion of Deuteronomy (ch. 16, v. 18 to ch. 21, v. 10) that speaks of the appointment of judges and the proper means of rendering judgment.

According to the science of astrology, a person under the influence of Virgo has a natural inclination to analyze phenomena in great detail, and sometimes to attach importance to minor details. There is a general tendency to perfectionism, constant introspection, and coldness toward emotion. These tendencies, when channeled through the Torah and its ways, enable a person to rectify himself in a most detailed way. However, if they are not channeled properly, these tendencies may lead to small-minded compulsiveness, worry, and lack of self-confidence.

The *Sefer Yetzirah* says, regarding this month, "In it, the Holy One, blessed be he, established the letter Yod as the king of the realm of action." During this month, one must resolve to make his actions coincide with his thoughts so that they may be as twins (Gemini ruled by Mercury) (see *Pri Tzadik,* beginning of discourse on Elul). The letter Yod symbolizes thought; correspondingly, it is with the letter Yod that the world-to-come (the future) is created. Therefore, through one's faculty of understanding (indicated in the first letter Heh of the divine Name; the letter that created this present world—see, in this book, the chapter on Nissan), one may lay the foundation of the world-to-come.

According to our Sages of blessed memory, the faculties of understanding and insight are feminine attributes. For this reason the sign of Virgo is symbolized by the feminine form.

The virgin symbolizes modesty and purity, essential traits of the true return to God.

The *Sefer Yetzirah* assigns the left hand (arm) to the month of Elul. The left, in this context, indicates materiality and action. These must be experienced bound to the letter Yod, to wisdom. Yod gave this month its form.

The full writing-out of the letters Yod, Yod, Vav, Daleth, expresses the path of enclosing wisdom in action. The letter Yod—symbolizing wisdom, connected with the letter Vav, the root of the attributes of communication and conjugation, and thereby connected with the letter Daleth—symbolizes the lowest realm of manifestation, the realm of action.

If one reads the letter Yod backwards, the word that the Yod, Vav, Daleth spells is *davay* (dire straits, uneasiness, worrisomeness), the result of not having used one's faculty of wisdom properly. From this we may be able to understand the association that the astrologers have made between this month and illnesses of the digestive system, such as ulcers. The energies of wisdom and analysis imparted by this sign's influence, if not used properly, may cause uneasiness and worry, because such a person is very sensitive to unwholesomeness.

This uneasy feeling makes Elul a month more urgently set aside for repentance, so as to return the order of the letters Daleth, Vav, Yod—*davay*—to Yod, Vav, Daleth, Yod, wisdom and life (for the word *chaim,* life, has the same numerical value as the word *hacham,* wise one).

After successfully working on the rectification of the faculty of hearing during the month of Av (Leo), which precedes the month of Elul, upon learning the lesson of future right action, from the travails that occurred in our history during the month of Av, we may arrive at a full appreciation of life (and wisdom), as it is written (Isaiah, ch. 55, v. 3), "Hear, and your soul shall live," for upon attaining a full understanding one may attain the wholesome life of the soul.

The heart (*lev,* the resting place of the soul), according to the explanation of the meaning of the letters by Rabbi Akiva (*Otyot d'Rabbi Akiva*), is symbolized by the letter Lamed, which in the *Sefer Yetzirah* is associated with the month of Tishrei (Libra), the month that follows Elul.

The mighty potential of rectification indicated within Elul was revealed to us by the collective work of penance on the part of the Jewish people in their desert wanderings. During Elul, Moses ascended Mount Sinai for a third time to intercede on behalf of the Jewish people so that Hashem would forgive them for the sin of the Golden Calf. By this process Moses opened the gates of penance for the month of Elul.

According to the Ari, the tribe that is associated with Elul is Gad. The Midrash states that the prophet Elijah hails from this tribe. Elijah, who is also referred to as the angel of the covenant, the source of holiness and purity, is associated with the attribute of *yesod* (foundation). The attribute *yesod* is the vessel of the covenant and is called *Tov* (good). The sign of this month, the virgin, is associated with this principle, as it is stated in Proverbs (ch. 18, v. 22), "Who finds a wife finds a great good (*tov*) and obtains favor from the Lord." Also, the name Gad is related by the *Magid Mesharim* to the attribute of *yesod* and to *tov* (goodness) (see *Bnei Yisaschar,* discourse on Elul, and *Magid Mesharim,* Shmoth).

Of the winter months, the month that corresponds to Elul is Adar (Pisces) whose sign is fish. The fish, whose source of existence is not separated from its environment, the waters, is a symbol of holiness and purity, and, therefore, of the sixth attribute, *yesod*. It is with this attribute that the sixth of the summer months (Elul) and the sixth of the winter months (Adar) culminate.

The letter Yod, whose numerical value is ten, denotes the full blossoming of summer. The letter Kof, that formed the month of Adar, has the numerical value of one hundred. It calls forth the end of the winter months, and its numerical value marks the completeness of both summer and winter—the general completeness.

As we have explained elsewhere in this book (see the chapters on Sivan and Kislev), the winter months complement and complete the summer months. During Adar we have the holiday of Purim, which is a time of the highest form of penance: return to God out of love for him. The month of Elul marks a lower form of penance: return to God out of his awesomeness. This is indicated by the month's letter, the Yod, which symbolizes wisdom, as it is written, "At the beginning of wisdom is fear of God (the appreciation of God's awesome majesty)" (Psalms, ch. 3, v. 10). This wisdom and appreciation of awe arises out of one's work of contemplation, the main spiritual service of this month.

During the month of Adar, the Jewish people accepted the Torah out of love for Hashem, for the Torah's sublime holiness was revealed to them through the miracle of Purim. This renewed acceptance brought about the great joy of the festival of Purim, when we festively eat, drink, and send presents. These activities are symbolized, according to the Talmud (Tractate *Shabbat,* 104a), by the letter Kof.

The combination of the divine Name associated with the month of Elul is Heh, Heh, Vav, Yod. The feminine letters, the two Hehs, precede the two masculine letters, Vav and Yod. This symbolizes the spiritual work from below, in order to arouse the divine response from above. The clear flow of Hashem's divine influence was interrupted by our sins, and is returned by our return from below to above. The process of this return is expressed in the verse from the Song of Songs (ch. 6, v. 3), "I am my beloved's and my beloved is mine"— "ani ledodi vidodi li," whose first letters form the name of the month, Elul.

The acceptance of God as one's ruler, and the contemplation of his ways, are symbolized by these two Hehs. The first Heh symbolizes *binah* (understanding); the second Heh symbolizes kingdom, the contemplation of *malchut.* These two together form the essential condition for true return of one's soul to its source. After one is successful, one merits the influence of Yod and Vav, the divine flow.

TISHREI
Libra (Scales)

The month of Tishrei was formed by means of the letter Lamed (ל), the tallest of all of the Hebrew letters. The astrological sign of this month is scales (Libra). The shape of the letter Lamed is similar to the form of balanced scales. The sign of this month indicates that, during this time, man's deeds are weighed upon scales. The tribe of this month is Ephraim (the son of Joseph). The combination of the letters of the divine Name, associated with this month is Vav, Heh, Yod, Heh. The essential nature of this month is symbolized in the image of sexual union.

The name of this month, Tishrei, indicates that it is the beginning of a new year for it contains the same letters as the word *bereshith* (beginning). The fact that the letters of the name Tishrei proceed in the opposite way of the natural order of the aleph-beth (Tav, the first letter, is the last letter of the aleph-beth; Shin, the next letter in Tishrei, is the second from the end, and similarly for the Resh) points to Tishrei as being a time of judgment. This is contrasted with the month of Nissan (where the letters do proceed in their natural order), which the Torah calls the month of *aviv* (spring), indicating that Nissan is a time of grace.

The meaning of the Aramaic word Tishrei is atonement. The atonement for deeds of the past enables a person to turn over a new leaf in life and begin afresh.

The letter Lamed, being the tallest of the aleph-beth, symbolizes the sublime opportunity that this month offers to a person, who may rise from the depths of sin to the greatest spiritual heights by setting his life in order and rectifying his heart. According to the *Otyot d'Rabbi Akiva,* the letter Lamed symbolizes *lev*—the heart.

The Lamed is one of the two central letters in the aleph-beth. It ends the letters of the right side (Aleph to Lamed), from which it can be seen to form the divine name El. It precedes the letters on the right side (Mem to Tav), whose combination forms the word *meth* (death). So, too, Tishrei marks the end of the first half of the year (which began with Nissan) and the beginning of the second half. It is regarded as the heart of the year, as the heart receives and distributes the spiritual energy for the entire year.

Following the month of Elul with its letter Yod, Tishrei with its letter Lamed combines with the Yod to form one word, li mine (unto me). This symbolizes the unification of God with his people in the image of a wedding, when the groom tells his bride, "Harei at mekudeshet li . . . ."—"You are now sacred unto me. . . ." The letters Lamed and Yod are the letters that begin and end the word "Israel," and symbolize this unity (see *Beni Yisarulam,* Discourse on Tishrei).

The essential nature of this month—mating, the intimate relationship between husband and wife—symbolizes the fact that during this month the unifying relationship between God and the Jewish people was formed. This is especially revealed on Yom Kippur, the tenth of Tishrei, when the two tablets containing the Ten commandments were given to us. This may be likened to a wedding gift: Just as a man acquires a wife by giving her a symbolic gift, and she understands that by accepting it she is consenting to marry him, so, too, with the giving of the Ten Commandments. (Note: This was the second time we received the Commandments, and, thus, this was the second marriage. The first marriage, upon receiving the first set of tablets on Shavuot, fifty days after Passover, was annulled on account of the sin of the Golden Calf.) Upon accepting the

Commandments, we became a nation of priests consecrated unto the Holy One, blessed be he. Thereby, we became the head of all nations.

This concept, as explained by the *Tikunei Zohar*, is contained in the name Israel, whose letters spell the word head (rosh), meaning that You (the nation of Israel) are a head unto Me (God); for the Jewish people are supposed to lead the world in the ways of God. This is the meaning of the verse (Exodus, ch. 19, v. 6), "And you shall become unto Me a nation of priests and a holy people."

According to the science of astrology, people born under the sign of Libra are especially blessed by harmonious and pleasurable feelings in connubial relationships. These blessings are refined and intensified by the opening of the spirit in relations between man and God, following the ways of the Torah.

Scales (Libra), the astrological symbol of this month, signifies the day of judgment that opens this month (Rosh Hashanah), and dictates a period of soul-searching, weighing the deeds of the past year. A person born under the sign of Libra is interested in many areas of endeavor and, thus, has difficulty in decision making. The commandments of the Torah facilitate one's ability to focus and organize, in the spirit of holiness, the complicated and confused energies of one's secular activities.

The element of this month is air, which it shares with the months Sivan and Shevat. It symbolizes the freshness and openness with which we receive the Torah. Whereas Tishrei was the month during which we received the second set of tablets, during Sivan we received the first set. During Shevat, Moses began to preach the book of Devarim, also called the Mishneh Torah (the review of the entire Torah). On the twenty-second day of Tishrei, we celebrate Simchat Torah, the joy of receiving the Torah. The element of air is composed of the balance of the two opposing elements, water and fire. The Torah is associated with these two elements.

Ephraim, the tribe of this month, symbolizes the energy of Joseph and the forebear of the Messiah of the house of Joseph, who, together with the Davidic Messiah of the house of Judah, will bring the complete redemption. This combination of Joseph and Judah is indicated in the relationship between the month of Nissan (whose tribe is Judah) and Tishrei (whose tribe is Ephraim). Each complements the other; the judgment of Tishrei is complemented by the grace of Nissan. Nissan is considered the first month in expression of the nature of God (so to speak), who first introduces to a person grace and kindness, thereby enabling him to be more easily meritorious in judgment.

This symbol of scales as a denotation of divine judgment is mentioned in the Pesikta (quoted by the commentary in the *Code of Jewish Law,* Orach Chaim, ch. 585, par. 1 of Rabbi Eliyahu of Vilna). On the sixth day of Creation, in the tenth hour, Adam was called to judgment for eating the fruit of the tree of knowledge. Then God told Adam, "Just as you are now standing before me in judgment, so, too, in all of the generations to come, your descendants shall stand before me in judgment on this day."

It is interesting to note that this Midrash adds weight to the theory of Rabbi Jonathan Eybeshitz, who said that at the time of Creation the earth moved around the sun at a much faster rate than it does now; for in the span of ninety-six hours, from the time of the creation of the stars to the tenth hour of the sixth day, at least six months had elapsed.

The heavenly body that rules Tishrei is Venus, which, according to the Talmud (*Shabbat,* 156a), causes the arousal of love and passion. These feelings are expressed in the Jewish calendar on the festival of Sukkot, which begins on the fifteenth of the month when the moon is full. The festival spans eight days. On the last day of the festival, Shemini Atzeret—Simchat Torah (the eighth day of Solemn Assembly—the Joy of the Torah), God and the Jewish people unite like a married couple.

The letter combination of the divine Name for this month is Vav, Heh, Yod, Heh. The last pair of letters—Vav, Heh—precedes the first pair—Yod, Heh—and thus calls attention to this month as the time of judgment. That the last two letters precede the first two indicates that it is left to the person on the earth below (symbolized by Vav, Heh) to be the first to arouse the Divine from above (symbolized by Yod, Heh). This is in contrast to the combinations of the Name for Nissan, which starts with Yod, Heh (above) and descends even to the unworthy, as it was when the children of Israel were liberated from Egyptian bondage (as Nissan is a period of divine grace).

The letters Vav, Heh, Yod, Heh spell the word *vehaya* (and it shall come to pass). This expression, when used in Scripture, always indicates good tidings (*Megilla,* 10b) and happiness. True happiness comes to a person only after he goes through a period of toil and judgment. Thus, the first half of the month of Tishrei is set aside for judgment, and the second half, which opens with Sukkot, is a time of rejoicing, culminating in Simchat Torah.

By means of this rejoicing, which is expressed in the Simchat Bet Hashoevah, the rite of drawing the water (for the altar of the Temple), one merits the drawing into oneself of the inspiration of the holy Spirit (*Sukkah,* 50b).

CHESHVAN
Scorpio (Scorpion)

The month of Cheshvan was formed by the letter Nun. Its nature is expressed by the sense of smell, and its sign is the scorpion. According to the Ari, its tribe is Menashe. In Jewish history, the most important event of this month was the completion of construction of the Temple of King Solomon, as it is written, "In the month of Bull, the eighth month from Nissan, the house was completed" (1 Kings, ch. 6, v. 38). Correspondingly, according to the Midrash, the Third Temple will be dedicated during this month. Just as the Tabernacle was completed during the month of Kislev and its dedication was four months later, during Nissan, and the Temple of Solomon was completed during Cheshvan and its dedication was eleven months later, in Tishrei, the Third Temple (may it be rebuilt soon) will be dedicated during Cheshvan. The future Third Temple is symbolized in the Hebrew word for the sign of Scorpio, *akrab*, which spells the words *ikar bet:* the essential house, which will never be destroyed.

The Hebrew name for this month, Bull (Cheshvan is the Aramaic name), calls our attention to the fact that the *mabul* (Flood) of Noah's generation began during this month. According to the Yalkut Shimoni, the fact that the letter Mem (of *mabul*) is missing in the month's name is explained by saying that *bull* actually means flood, and that the letter Mem preceding it,

59

containing the numerical value of forty, indicates that the flood lasted for forty days (lasting from the seventeenth of Marcheshvan until the twenty-seventh of Kislev). Each year following the Flood, the world felt the residual catastrophic effects of the Flood, and people were in a state of panic. However, with the dedication of the Temple of Solomon during Cheshvan, these residual catastrophes ceased. The Flood is also hinted at in the word *akrab* (Scorpio), in that the scorpion's bite inevitably is *oker bet* (destroys the house).

This contrast between destruction and fall, on the one hand, and construction and essential stability, on the other, is a prominent theme of this month and is revealed through the letter Nun. In its negative aspect, the letter Nun is first in the word *nefilah* (fall). Therefore, in King David's prayer Ashrei (Psalms, 145), which praises God according to the aleph-beth, the verse of the letter Nun does not appear. Instead, the next letter takes over and sings, "Somech Hashem lechol hanoflim"—"God supports those who fall." The letter Nun, with its numerical value of fifty, in this context represents the fifty gates of impurity. For this reason the verse referring to such a fall was omitted, for such a fall, clearly expressed, cannot return of its own accord.

The source of the fifty gates of holiness is the neshamah (soul). The letters of *neshamah* indicate this: Nun is fifty, and *shamah* means her name. The *neshamah,* which also may be taken to mean the breath, is bound up with the nose (and thus with the sense of smell, the attribute of the month); as it is written, "and He blew into his nostrils *nishmath chaim* (the breath of life) and man became a living being" (Genesis, ch. 2, v. 1). At the end of the Sabbath we make *havdalah*—the conscious separation between sacred and profane. During this ritual we partake of a pleasant-smelling spice in order to strengthen the *neshamah,* which just left the blessed realm of the Sabbath in order to face the week. The sense of smell is considered the most spiritual of the senses because the *neshamah* derives its substance most directly from it. The sense of smell, directly connected with the soul's intuition, is the faculty by which we precipitate either ultimate victory or its opposite.

Associated with the month of Cheshvan and the Flood of Noah is the sense of smell, as mentioned in the Torah upon Noah's rescue, when he offered up a sacrifice: "And God smelled the pleasant fragrance" (Genesis, ch. 8, v. 21). The sense of smell, so intimately connected with the soul, is revealed in the tribe of this month, Menasheh, whose name contains the same letters as *neshamah,* in a different arrangement (see *Bnei Yisaschar,* Discourse on Cheshvan).

The letters that form the name Cheshvan are close to those that form the word *heshbon* (making a clear accounting), whose root is the power of intentional thought formed in the soul, whose resting place is in the mind.

The element of this month, water, is a clear association with the catastrophic Flood, when the water destroyed the world.

The heavenly body that influences Cheshvan is Mars, associated with the principle of stern judgment. The judgment visited upon the world by the Flood occurred as a result of the world's misuse of the power of desire, which is rooted in the element of water. This pollution of the water element brought about the retribution by this element.

The generation of the Flood was, according to our Sages, potentially fit for receiving the Torah and the rendition of its deepest secrets. However, due to their sinfulness, they transformed the blessed waters of the Torah's wisdom and grace to the bitter water of sin.

According to the science of astrology, a person born under the influence of the sign Scorpio has an extremely powerful emotional sensitivity, and an equally powerful natural inclination. These features, if not used properly, may lead one to the depths of depravity. However, on the positive side, a person with such powerful sensitivities has the ability to penetrate directly to the deepest appreciation of values, and, if his will is so directed, he may achieve a deep understanding of the Torah.

The divine service of this month is one's full acceptance of the decrees of heaven as revealed in the Torah. This calls for an appreciation of the awesomeness of heaven. Through such contemplative means (symbolized by the letter Nun, pointing to the fifty gates of purity or its opposite), one may be delivered from the evil and destructiveness associated with this month.

Cheshvan, the second of the winter months, is complemented by the second summer month, Iyar. The attribute of that month is thought, and its form of worship is awe and power. They are completed by the spiritual work of the month of Cheshvan, which is the acceptance, out of appreciation, of awe and the yoke of the kingdom of heaven.

According to Rabbi Menachem of Rimanov, in the course of Jewish history, there were recurrent decrees by the Jewish host countries during this month that resulted in the confiscation of Jewish property. The cause of these decrees was the revolt on the part of the Jewish people against the sovereignty of the Davidic throne, when many tribes accepted the kingdom of Jeroboam of the tribe of Ephraim. During Cheshvan he created a holiday for his constituents in order to lure them away from the pilgrimage to Jerusalem.

The source of Jeroboam's revolt was envy and baseless hatred. These sins eventually brought about the destruction of the Second Temple. The rectification of this sin will result in the building of the Third holy Temple and its inauguration, which will occur during the month of Cheshvan.

During the month of Shevat, Moses, in his fortieth year as leader of the Jewish people in the desert, began the book of Deuteronomy. The source of this pouring forth of the waters of Torah was the sign of that month, the pitcher of Aquarius. This is related to the Torah that will be revealed during the Messianic era, which will proceed from the "name" of the month of Av, symbolizing the Father, and the attribute of wisdom and springtime (*aviv*) that will be revealed during this month.

The fifteenth of Shevat marks the drawing of a new period of the year, and is the beginning of the new year for the planting of trees (and for tithes, etc.). Similarly, the fifteenth of Av marks the foreshadowing of the new year that begins on the first of Tishrei. Between the fifteenth of Av and Rosh Hashanah (the new year of Tishrei) is a period of forty-five days of preparation until the beginning of Nissan. The word *adam* (man) has the numerical value of 45; thus, this period is the time when man makes himself more human, completes his God-like image.

Both Av and Shevat come after the end of the first third of the year. Av is four months after Nissan; Shevat, four months after Tishrei. The first third of the year corresponds to the upper third of the body, the head. The beginning of this second third corresponds to the second third of the body, which contains the heart (see *Chidushei HaRim* on the fifteenth of Shevat). For the month of Av, this corresponds to the sign Leo; for the month of Shevat, it corresponds to the new year of the trees.

KISLEV
Sagittarius (Bow)

Regarding the month of Kislev, the following is stated in the *Sefer Yetzirah,* attributed to our Patriarch Abraham: "He coronated it with the letter Samech in the attribute of sleep; attached a crown to it and forged them together and formed within them the bow (Sagittarius) in the worldly realm, Kislev in the realm of time (the year), and the stomach within the microcosmic realm, in the male and female."

Rabbi Zaddok Hakohen (*Pri Tzadik,* Genesis, Rosh Chodesh Kislev) says that the name Kislev denotes confidence and inner strength, as used in the verse (Job, ch. 31, v. 24), "If I have made gold my hope (*kisli*) and have said to the fine gold, 'You are my confidence.'" (It is interesting to note that in English the word castle, composed of the same phonetics as the Hebrew *kesel,* means fortress.) The word *kesel* is etymologically related to the word *kisuy,* covering and guarding. According to the Ibn Ezra (ibid.), the word *kesel* means a walking staff or crutch. According to Rashi, *kesel* means the hope that comes from planning, as in the verse, "For God will be your support (bekislecha)." The advisors of the body are the kidneys (*kelayot*), which are related to the word *kala,* which means strong desire and longing. Thus, the main spiritual functions of the month of Kislev are the strengthening of faith in God and the affirmation of hope in complete liberation.

These themes that derive from the word Kislev come to expression in the holiday of Chanukah, which begins on the twenty-fifth of Kislev. On that day the Hashmonaim, placing their trust in the power of God, merited the victory of crushing the imperial influence of the Hellenists. Their strong desire for purity and holiness achieved its goal, culminating in the miracle of the jar of pure oil that burned for eight days although it was only enough for one.

The attributes and images of Kislev, confidence and the fortress, are also indicated in the letter of the month, Samech, whose form is a closed circle, symbolizing protection. The word Samech also means support and reestablishment. These attributes are available to us during the month of Kislev.

According to the science of astrology, a person born under the sign of Sagittarius has much self-confidence, is optimistic, and is always pressing ahead. His hope for the future arouses within him the inner resolve to overcome the obstacles standing in his way and carries him until he achieves his goal.

These virtues achieved full expression in the campaign of the Hashmonaim (against the more numerous and powerful Greco-Syrian Hellenists), for their willingness to give their lives in the hope of success, for their staunch self-determination in the face of the Greek Empire, whose cultural values placed a premium on physical pleasure (and who used astrology mainly to achieve that end).

For the believing Jew, the constellations of the heavens are there to teach a person how to achieve spiritual elevation in consonance with the spiritual significance of each of the astrological signs. These signs were explained by our holy Sages in the *Zohar* and Kabbalah. These constellations may be likened to the physical body, which enables the soul inhabiting it to achieve many significant things in its life.

The person whose sign is Sagittarius is armed with the energies of the soul that enable him to achieve sublime spiritual heights if mobilized in the ways of the Torah. If a person uses these energies for purely material purposes, his soul powers

will not bring him wholesome happiness and spiritual fulfillment, but rather their opposites.

One example of the Sagittarian personality discussed in
astrology books is the philosopher Baruch Spinoza. His history
may serve to exemplify some of the negative derivations of the
Sagittarian personality; his soul potential was great, but he
used it in ways not consistent with the inner truth. In Spinoza's
life, the Sagittarian expertise expressed itself in the travails of
wandering about and in confused interaction with society. This
type of misuse of Sagittarian energy affects not only one's spiritual equilibrium, but also one's harmony.

According to the Shem MiShmuel (*Chayei Sarah*), Sagittarius the bow symbolizes the power of prayer that issues from
the depths of the heart and pierces the upper heavens. As a
bow issues forth an arrow, the tighter the arrow presses against
the bow; and, when being aimed at the heavens, the closer the
arrow is to earth, the higher it will travel when it is released.

This analogy explains the situation of the Jews of the up-
rising of the Hashmonaim. The Greco-Syrian Empire op-
pressed the Jewish nation greatly by its laws designed to
forcibly enculturate and subdue the Jewish people. This led to
the mobilization of the inner sparks of the souls of the Jewish
people and to the formation of the Hashmonean kingdom
under the leadership of Matityahu.

The bow, as a symbol of the power of prayer, is found in
the Onkelos's translation of Jacob's words to Joseph (Genesis,
ch. 18, v. 22), "That I conquered from the hands of the Emorite
with my sword and bow," which Onkelos translates as "prayer."

The revelation of the inner resolve of the Jewish nation in
the time of the Hashmonaim is also indicated in the word
Kislev, etymologically related to the words *kesalim* (loins); *kelayot* (kidneys—advice); and *keliya* (intense longing). It points
to the intense longing of the Jewish people for holiness and
purity, which was evident in the successful revolt. These qualities are available each year, as the yearly cycle reaches the
holiday of Chanukah this month. The word Chanukah, related
to the word *chinuch,* meaning renewal (proper education,

rededication), symbolizes these attributes in the issuance from the depths of the heart of the purpose of self-sanctification and renewal.

When these energies are used in a non-spiritual way, they are expressed in the desire for adventure and an inclination toward powerful experiences which, if not channeled in spiritual awareness, may cause harm to the Sagittarian. In the practice of Judaism, these spiritual powers come to expression in the rituals of the Chanukah festival.

The nature of this month, as mentioned before, is sleep. This is a negative expression of this month's energy, the natural state of spiritual slumber. This was the situation the Jews found themselves in under the dominion of the Greek Empire, and it was particularly in this state that the inner essence of the Jews was aroused, as in the verse (*Song of Songs,* ch. 5, v. 2), "I am asleep but my heart is awake."

This theme—the ability to be roused from spiritual sleep —is indicated in the words of *Sefer Yetzirah:* "He coronated the letter Samech in the attribute of sleep." The power of support and renewal, symbolized in the letter Samech, which roused the inner will and confidence, overcame spiritual slumber and dormancy.

The element of Kislev, fire, also expresses the power of rising upward that is the essence of this month. It is also the central motif of the Chanukah ritual: the kindling of the festival lights.

The spiritual tendencies of rising above the mundane, spiritual alertness, and a natural inclination to the study of philosophy and religion are also among the attributes assigned to the Sagittarian by astrology. They reach their full expression in the fulfillment of the Torah and its ways.

Astrology orders the month of Sagittarius in the category of the changing months. This implies that Sagittarius carries with it the possibility of change, as was revealed during Chanukah, when the spiritual situation of the Jewish people changed from slumber and negative self-image to renewal and revitalization.

It is interesting to note that the three other changing months—Sivan, Elul, and Adar—all carry within them symbols of change essential to Jewish practice. The month of Sivan saw the giving of the Torah, which was the most fundamental change within the Jewish nation, transforming them from a nation of slaves to a kingdom of princes, a holy nation. The month of Elul is set aside for repentance, for the mending of one's ways. During this month the essential purity of the Jewish people was returned to them, after being tainted as a result of the sin of the Golden Calf.

The last of the changing months, Adar, saw the change of decree from annihilation to life and liberation during the days of Esther and Mordechai, in the last days of the Persian exile. The month was changed from a time of mourning to a time of great rejoicing.

The bow, the sign of this month, may be seen as a symbol of the victory of the Jewish people against Greco-Syrian domination, as it is written in the verse (Zachariah, ch. 1, v. 13), "For I have bent Judah for me, I have filled the bow with Ephraim and raised up my sons against thy sons, on Greece and made thee as the sword of a mighty man."

Greece symbolizes the opposing negative power of the bow; the bow of Greece was aimed at the bow of Israel. This bow symbolizes materialistic philosophy, which was the cornerstone of Greek culture as it sought to destroy the faith and torch of Israel. The Greek attempt to desecrate the holiness of Israel aroused the Maccabean revolt, which saw the triumph of the bow of holiness over the bow of impurity. The ancients say that the fall of Greek culture, with its emphasis on intellectual wisdom, brought about the rise of the development of the Oral tradition of the Torah, which was catalyzed during that time. The bow of Judah swallowed the wisdom of Greece and sanctified it.

This idea is implied in the letters that form the word *tsiyon* (Zion), which is made up of the letter Tzadi and the letters Yod, Vav, Nun, which spell the word Yavan (Greece). The zaddik, the holy man, rules over the attribute of *yavan* (worldly knowledge). According to astrology, the heavenly body that rules over the constellation of Sagittarius is Jupiter (in Hebrew, *Zedek,* meaning righteousness). In the days of Chanukah, the righteousness and purity of the Jewish people were proved for all to see.

In the mystical symbolism of Kabbalah (See *Kehilat Yaakov,* section on Hetz), the bow comes with three arrows, which symbolize either the triplets grace, judgment, and harmony; or victory, glory, and foundation; or wisdom, understanding, and knowledge. These attributes are symbolized in the first three letters of the divine Name (Yod, Heh, Vav), which also appear at the end of the name of the Maccabee leader Matityahu; by the holiness and power of these letters, Matityahu was able to overcome the Greek forces. The three letters Yod, Heh, and Vav correspond to the letters Yod, Vav, Nun (Yavan, or Greece) in that the Nun (fifty) is ten times the Heh (five), and the Yod and Vav are the same in both. The three evil arrows of Yod, Vav, Nun were defeated by the three holy arrows of Yod, Heh, Vav, delivered by Matityahu and his followers.

According to the Talmud (*Megilla,* 16b) the word "honor" refers to the *tefillin* that a person puts on his head. The connection to the supernal source offered by the *tefillin* is available to us through the rituals associated with the festival of Purim, whereby one transcends the physical plane and finds true happiness.

The relation between the months of Kislev and Adar, expressed by their sharing the same ruling heavenly body, *Zedek* (Jupiter), with all its ramifications, is also indicated by the meaning of the names of these months: security and strength. Both of these attributes are evident in the events leading to the institution of the festivals of Chanukah and Purim. The similarity of these months is also evident in their both being associated with Joseph the righteous.

In Aramaic (the language of ancient Babylon), the language in which we have the names of the months, the meaning of the word Adar is the mast of a boat, which uses the wind (*ruach* means both wind and spirit) to travel on the sea. This symbolizes the power of this month, during which one is able to withstand any spirit that interferes with the path of the Torah (see *Chidushei HaRim,* Adar). Perhaps it is from this connection that astrology describes the Piscean as being tolerant and able to withstand difficult circumstances. However, without the guidance of Torah, this character trait may lead a person to misfortune and depression resulting from personal failure.

In Aramaic, another implication of the word Adar is "hidden miracle"; during the month of Adar, indeed, the miracle of Purim was hidden in natural circumstances. However, Nissan, meaning open miracles (*nissim* means miracles) is a time of revealed miracles, such as occurred during our liberation from Egypt. The Aramaic language is closely related to the Hebrew —i.e., the Hebrew meanings of our words are hidden in the Aramaic. Thus, Adar, with its hidden miracle, expresses its meaning in Aramaic; Nissan, with its revealed miracles, expresses its meaning in Hebrew (see *Chidushei HaRim,* ibid.).

The combination of letters of the divine Name, as it is associated with this month, is Heh, Heh, Yod, Vav. The feminine, symbolized by the two Hehs, precedes the masculine, symbolized by the Yod and Vav. This is similar to the month of Elul, where the combination of the divine Name is Heh, Heh, Vav, Yod. Both indicate the return of Israel (symbolized by the feminine, receptive Hehs) to God (symbolized by the masculine, active Yod and Vav). During Adar this is revealed in the return to God out of love; during Elul the return to God is due to the appreciation of his awesome transcendence. These combinations precede the combinations for Nissan and Tishrei, where the former corresponds to divine grace and the latter to divine judgment.

The impurity of the Greek bow is indicated in the prayer of Hannah (1 Samuel, ch. 2, v. 4): "The bows of the mighty men are broken and they that stumbled are girded with strength," which the Targum Yonatan ben Uziel (rabbinic translation into Aramaic) renders as referring to the bow of the Greeks, which was conquered by the Hashmonaim, the Maccabees.

The three arrows and their connection with the bow are associated, according to Kabbalah, with the relationship between King David and his friend Jonathan, when Jonathan tells David (1 Samuel, ch. 20, v. 20), "I will shoot three arrows on the side, as though I shot them at a target." According to Kabbalah, Jonathan possesses the soul of the Messiah from the house of Joseph. This is indicated in his Hebrew name Yehonatan (containing the letters Yod, Heh, Vav, which also appear in one of the spellings of the name of Joseph, Yehoseph, as in the verse (Psalms, ch. 81, v. 6), "This He ordained in Yehoseph for testimony. . . ."

Joseph is also associated with the sign of Sagittarius, as it is written (Genesis, ch. 49, v. 24), "His bow dwelt in strength." His three arrows, the Yod, Heh, Vav, were revealed within Jonathan and Matityahu. The victories of Joseph over the impurity of Egypt, and of tsiyon (Zion) over Greece, both associated with the bow of Sagittarius, are seen as identical to each other, as the numerical value of Joseph is equivalent to that of Zion (156).

The three arrows of the bow correspond to the three prongs of the letter Shin (ש), which also symbolizes the three attributes mentioned previously. According to the *Sefer Yetzirah,* it was with the letter Shin that the element of fire (*esh*) was created. From here we may see the connection between the element of fire and the sign of Sagittarius. Joseph, whose sign is Sagittarius, exemplifies the power of fire, as is written in the verse (Obadiah, ch. 1, v. 18), "And the house of Joseph shall be as a flame." The letter Shin, with its three prongs, also symbolizes harmony and righteousness. The divine attribute *yesod* (foundation) is the source of energy for the sign of Sagittarius.

Sleep, the natural attribute of the month of Kislev, symbolizes, according to Rabbi Zaddok Hakohen, the vision and understanding that one may attain through dreams, just as King Solomon attained his great wisdom through a dream. The power of dreams is revealed in Joseph, the master of dreams. The Hebrew word for dream, *chalom,* has the numerical value of 78, three times the value of the divine Name (Yod, Heh, Vav,

Heh), which has the value of 26. The three times the divine Name refers to the three attributes *netzach, hod,* and *yesod* (victory, glory, and foundation), which are also symbolized by the three arrows of the bow.

This energy of the bow, as expressed in the dreams of Joseph, which are associated with sleep, the attribute of Kislev, expresses the essential nature of this sign. According to the science of astrology, Sagittarians have natural psychic ability, which enables them to anticipate the thoughts of others and to attain mastery over the forces of nature. These abilities were fully expressed in the personality of Joseph.

The potential for righteousness is highly developed among Sagittarians. Their opinions are built on the pillars of sincere investigation and understanding, as Pharaoh said to Joseph: "Since God has shown all of this to you, there is none so discrete and wise as you."

The bow is also a symbol for the attribute of *yesod* (foundation), the sixth attribute of the emotive spheres (see *Kehilat Yaakov,* entry for *keshet*). *Yesod* is Joseph's attribute. It is symbolized in the Vav of the divine Name (whose numerical value is 6). The form of the Vav (ו) calls to mind the arrow, and it is in this form that astrology symbolizes Sagittarius. The Hebrew word for arrow, *hetz,* also indicates its association with the attribute of *yesod,* for it has the numerical value of the words *yesod chai*—living foundation. (See ibid., entry for *hetz.*) The letters Het and Tzadi by themselves also symbolize *yesod:* Het stands for Chaim (life), and Tzadi means righteousness.

The foundation of life is also indicated in the numerical value of the Hebrew word for bows (*keshe*): Kuf—100, Shin—300, Tav—400 = 800; 100 (10 × 10) times 8. Eight, as we mentioned earlier, is the symbol for life, and 100 symbolizes the essential unity within diversity. The numerical value of the word *yesod* is 80. This indicates a clear connection between *yesod* and the bow (10 × 80 = 800). It symbolizes the process of drawing life-energy from the highest source of life-energy (8 × 10 = 80 × 10 = 800) to the foundation (80) that gives energy to the more immediate manifestation of life (8). The connection of these processes is symbolized by the arrow, the astrological symbol of Sagittarius.

According to astrology, the Sagittarian is full of appreciation and joy in life, as indicated by the essential connection Sagittarius has to life-energy. However, this comes about only if one's lifestyle is in accord with the spiritual values of Torah. If one's lifestyle is essentially secular, the Sagittarian energy expresses itself as irritability, and a person may also find himself in dangerous circumstances due to the negative expression of the adventurous tendencies of the Sagittarian.

The letters of the word *keshet* (bow), according to the numerological formulation of Alef, Yod, Kuf (1, 10, 100), Bet Kaf Resh (2, 20, 200), form the word *eged,* the knot (which binds separate entities together), symbolizing unity. This indicates the Sagittarian potential to unify masses of people, and points to Joseph, who unified Egypt in the face of danger and achieved unity with his brothers, and to the Messiah of the house of Joseph, who gathers together and unifies the Jewish people. The word Joseph is etymologically related to the word *asifa* (gathering together).

Sagittarians enjoy an easygoing nature that is naturally conducive to cordial relations between people. They also have the ability to draw people to their will. These traits were also exemplified in Joseph. The Sagittarian's personable nature is also indicated in the Hebrew word *keshet* (bow), which is related to the word *lekasher,* to tie together.

The harmony implicit in Sagittarius is related to the word *keshet,* which also means rainbow, where the natural colors are harmonically displayed. According to Kabbalah, the three main colors of the rainbow—white, red, and yellow-green—symbolize the three attributes grace, judgment, and beauty, or the three attributes victory, glory, and foundation (see *Sefat Emet* of Menachem Azaria of Fano). Three of the elements are also derived from the *keshet* and its colors; if we were to use the numerological device Aleph, Yod, Kof; Bet Kof Resh (1, 10; 2, 20, 200), the Kof would become an Aleph, and would symbolize air (*Avir*), which, in the light of the sun, contains a yellowish hue. *Tiferet* (beauty), the Shin, according to the *Sefer Yetzirah,* symbolizes fire (*Esh*) and is associated with the color red (*Gevurah*—power, judgment). The Tav would be transformed into a Mem, since Tav has the numerical value of 400 and Mem has the value of 40. Mem symbolizes water (*mayim*) and is given the color white (*Chesed*—grace).

The rainbow (*keshet*) symbolizes the essential ingredients of form. This concept is derived from the letters that come after the word Keshet—Kof, Resh and Shin, Tav; Tav, the last letter, would become an Aleph, the first letter, and together they would from the word *toar,* form. This points to the pleasing disposition of the Sagittarians, as Joseph is described as "Yefe toar vyafe mareh"—"A pleasant form and beautiful to look upon" (Genesis, ch. 39, v. 6). Astrology also describes the Sagittarian as being a pleasant form and a strong, athletically built body. Aleph, Resh, Tav also symbolizes the lights of Chanukah (Orot), and thereby the light of the Oral tradition, which was stimulated by the Hashmonean victory.

The *Bnei Yisaschar* explains that the connection between light, Torah, and the bow is the reason for the custom of shooting arrows on the holiday of Lag b'Omer (the thirty-third day of the Omer, during the month of Iyar), the day of the passing of Rabbi Shimon bar Yochai. On that day, before his death, Rabbi Shimon revealed many important secrets of Kabbalah (see *Zohar,* vol. 3, 176). The revelation of the hidden light may be likened to the shining forth of the colors of the rainbow. Rabbi Shimon told his son, Rabbi Eleazar, "My son, do not expect the coming of the Messiah until you see the self-illuminated rainbow." Thus, the coming of the Messiah is likened to the revelation of the hidden light. Chanukah, according to Kabbalah, is also, with the kindling of the lights, a symbol of the illumination of the hidden light.

According to the *Bnei Yisaschar,* Jacob's son Yissachar, whose birth occurred on the holiday of Shavuot, was conceived on Chanukah. This symbolizes the essential connection between Chanukah and Torah, as expressed in the verse, "And the children of Yissachar, the knowers of understanding of the times," and is mirrored in the traditional Chanukah hymn (Ma'oz Tzur), "Children of understanding these eight days . . . ."

The relationship between Shavuot, when the Torah was given, and Chanukah, when the tradition of the Torah was reawakened, may be understood according to the principle of the Ari (Rabbi Yitzchak Luria, Kabbalist of Safed, sixteenth century), who says that the twelve months are divided into the six summer months, which are called the months of the divine feminine (passive) embodiment, and the six winter months, the divine masculine (active) embodiment. Thus, the third of the summer months, Sivan, which is connected with light, symbolizes both the light of the sun and the light of Torah. The third winter month, Kislev, also has symbolism involving light: the rainbow, which symbolizes the hidden light of the developmental Oral tradition.

The bow, as a symbol of the holiness of the attribute of *yesod* (foundation), is seen in the *keshet,* Kof Sheth. Kof, in the Talmud (Tractate *Shabbat,* 104b) is an acronym for *kedusha* (holiness), and Sheth in Aramaic means six—i.e., the sixth attribute, *yesod.*

In the Aleph → Yod → Kof, Beth → Kof → Resh manipulation of words, the word *Keshet* (קשת) is transformed into the divine name Shaddai (שדי), meaning, "God who expresses his infinity within limitation" (see *Kehilat Yaakov,* Shaddai), and also is associated with the *yesod,* the masculine generation principle. The masculine gender, *zachar,* is also related to the word *zach* (pure).

The letters after the word *zachar* (Zayin, Kof, Resh)—Heth, Lamed, Shin—spell the word *shelach*—the sprung arrow, symbolizing Sagittarius. The word *zachar* also means remembrance, symbolizing the three essential mitzvot that the Hellenists forbade: circumcision, the Sabbath, and Torah study, which are called spiritual remembrances. The Hashmonaim revived these three mitzvot, which may be likened to the three arrows of the bow.

The divine name Shaddai, associated earlier with Sagittarius, is also equivalent to the Tzadi (צדי) (Tzadi, Daleth, Yod) if we switch the Shin with the (צדי) Tzadi, both being dental–labial letters (see *Sefer Yetzirah*). Thus, we may observe the symbol for *yesod,* Zaddik (the righteous), and also the ruling planet of Sagittarius, Zedek, Jupiter. We may also observe the essential connection the astrologers have pointed out between proper interpersonal behavior (*tzedek*) and Sagittarius.

(קשת) Keshet, which, with the A → Y → K, B → C → R equivalence, is also the word (קדש) *kadosh* (holy), symbolizes the summit of holiness revealed by Joseph, who maintained his spiritual integrity even within the decadent Egyptian society.

The unholy manifestation of *keshet,* the power of lust, impure grace, is symbolized by Ishmael, about whom the Torah says, "And he became an archer (*rove kashat*)" (Genesis, ch. 21, v. 20). Joseph was sold to the Ishmaelites, the impure bow, and brought to Egypt, the "decadence of the land." According to the Midrash, Greece is also symbolized by the bow, as seen in the verse when Isaac told Esau, "Take your quiver and your bow" (Genesis, ch. 27, v. 3); the bow refers to Greece.

Arav, the generic name of the Ishmaelites, also symbolizes *yesod,* for it is related to the word *eruv,* the common association of the multitude, just as *yesod* gathers together all the attributes of both the left and right sides of the tree of life. Here we see the contrast between the holy and unholy Sagittarius.

The multitude of colors of the rainbow symbolizes the realm of desire (*hakeshet,* the bow, has the same letters as the word *hatshuka,* the desire—longing). The realm of desire has the power to raise one to the heights of spirituality or to lower one to the depths of materiality. The word *arev* also means sublime (spiritual) pleasure; if used in a mundane way, it connotes the awakening of domesticity: *ar*— awaken, *bet*—house.

According to Rabbenu Bachaya (see his commentary on the Torah [Deuteronomy, ch. 31, v. 16], the Ishmaelite lands are ruled by the sign of Scorpio—*akrab,* which connotes the negative association *akar bet,* destroying the house (domestic tranquility), and points to the destruction of the world, the great Flood that occurred during the month of Cheshvan, whose sign is Scorpio. The flood was brought about by an overabundance of desire—passion that was channeled into sinfulness. During that month the flood both began and ended, and the rainbow was shown to Noah as he descended from the ark on the seventeenth of the month.

Cheshvan, the second of the winter months, corresponds to Iyar, the second of the summer months. On the eighteenth of Iyar (Lag b'Omer), the custom is to shoot bows and arrows in honor of Rabbi Shimon bar Yochai, who was said to have incorporated all of the colors of the rainbow.

The negative connotation of *keshet,* Kof Sheth, is derived from the *Zohar* (Teruma, Vol. 2), where the letter Kof is said to symbolize the ape (in Hebrew, *kof*), the lower man, and Sheth, the attribute of *yesod* (the lower man ruling over the *yesod*). *Keshet* can also be taken as Kash Tav, where according to the explication of the letters of Rabbi Akiva (Otyot d'Rabbi Akiva), the Tav symbolizes desire—lust (*taavah*), and Kash, the *chaf* (the *chaf* of desire).

According to Kabbalah, the month of Kislev is associated with the Matriarch Rachel, about whom the Torah says, upon the birth of her son Benjamin, "Vatekash beliditah"—"And she was in hard labor." The word *vatekash* has the same letters as *keshet*. Similarly, the Shem MiShmuel (Chayei Sarah, vol. 1, Rosh Chodesh Kislev) says that Hannah (mother of the prophet Samuel) symbolizes the bow, as she said to Eli, the High Priest, who mistook her for drunk because of the way she was praying, "Ki isha keshat ruach anochi"—"For I am a woman of troubled spirit" (1 Samuel, ch. 1, v. 16). With her prayer, from the depths of her heart, Hannah pierced the heavens, just as the arrow travels further the more pressure there is on the bow.

The heavenly rainbow is a result of the reflection of the light of the sun on the moisture in the air. This symbolizes the process of sublimation of desire. Just as the arrows of the bow pierce the material mundaneness, so, too, the light of Kislev broke the hold of the Syrian Hellenists, and the bow of the righteous emerged victorious.

According to the Ari, the month of Kislev corresponds to the tribe of Benjamin, who was born to Rachel after a hard and fatal labor. Benjamin the righteous completed the process started by Joseph when he descended to Egypt. In the encampment formation of the Jews' wandering in the desert, the tribe of Benjamin was at the rear of Joseph's encampment. Joseph had two tribes named after his two sons: Ephraim, at the head, whose month is Tishrei; and Menashe, whose month is Cheshvan.

The idea of the sign of the bow, and the implication of the hopeful, faithful yearning of the soul carried in the name of the month Kislev, etymologically related to the word *kilayon* (pining), is revealed during Chanukah, as the *Sefat Emet* says, responding to the verses in the Psalms (ch. 40, v. 2–3): "I waited patiently for God and he inclined toward me and heard my cry. He brought me out of the desolate tumultuous pit, from the mire of Yavan (the literal translation is "from the miry clay"). He set my feet on a rock and balanced my steps."

The faith of Israel in God, and the yearning of their soul for holiness, lifted them like an arrow pushing forth from a bow; from the depths of decadent materialism that was Greco-Syrian culture. The Greek oppression of the inner soul of Israel aroused the essence of the soul, the point of the Zaddik, the righteous. The root of the life force of the Zaddik pierced, like an arrow, the impurity and spiritual emptiness. This process is contained in the word *hetz* (arrow), in the letters (חת—צידק) Heth—Tzadi (צדיק), that form it. These letters symbolize life (*chayut*) and righteous works (*tzedakot*). When fully spelled out (Heth, Tav, Tzadi, Daleth, Yod, Kof), their numerical value is 612, the same as the word *Berit,* the covenant and the power of rising up.

The inner arousal out of the depths of iniquity constitute the hidden light that is especially revealed during Chanukah. Those whose deeds are worthy can perceive it in the lights of Chanukah.

The bow (*keshet*) and its relation to the attribute of *yesod* is revealed in the rearrangement of its letters to form the word (שתק) *shotek* (being silent), for the attribute of *yesod* expresses itself in its ability to preserve the inner secret in purity of speech. It is interesting that the Hebrew word for "word"—*milah*—is the same as the word for the covenant of circumcision. This power of silence characterized not only our Matriarch Rachel and Joseph and Benjamin, her two sons, but also Queen Esther, a descendant of Rachel. The word *shotek,* can be Shet Kof, 6 (*yesod,* the sixth attribute) and its foundation in holiness (*kedusha*). The silence of Rachel and her offspring guarded the existence and continuation of the Jewish nation, which was established in the power of the guarded secret and is charged to be circumspect in the revelation of secrets (see the Maharal's commentary on the Torah, beginning of Exodus). The word *yesod* is composed of the Yod, symbolizing wisdom, and *sod,* secret, the secret wisdom.

If one succeeds in keeping silent properly, it results in finding favor in people's eyes, as we see in the stories of both Joseph and Esther. This is shown in the word composed of the letters following the word (שתק) *shotek,* using the A → Y → K, B → K → R transposition, the word (תאר) *toar,* (balanced) form. Both Joseph and Rachel were found, by the Scriptures, to be of well-balanced form. Their faces drew freely from the inner hidden depths of their souls in their full manifestation of the *keshet* (rainbow).

Astrology describes well-aligned Sagittarians as possessing inner strength and control over their impulses, as free from anger and rage as a still pool whose waters run deep. Only extenuating circumstances bring the Sagittarian to an outbreak of anger, but even then his anger soon quiets down. This is similar to the nature of an arrow: The greater the inner impression it makes on the bow, the greater the force with which it shoots forth. This image of "shooting forth" was revealed in its holy form during Chanukah, for during the time of the festival's founding, the secret soul of Israel sprang forth, under the guidance of Matityahu and his children, against the spiritual darkness of Greece.

The sign of the bow deeply influences the months that follow immediately after—Tevet, Shevat, and Adar. This is evident also in the names of the signs and their relation to the word *keshet* (bow). The *gdee* (goat), Capricorn—Tevet; the *dlee* (pitcher of water, or water carrier), Aquarius—Shevat; and *dagim* (fishes), Pisces—Adar, each have essential attributes that are found in the *keshet,* Sagittarius. Each of these are composed of letters that are derived from *keshet* in the A → Y → K, B → K → R transposition: Kof, Yod; Tav, Daleth, Mem; Shin, Lamed, Gimel—(קשת—גדי—דלי—דגים).

Capricorn (*gdee,* the goat), the sign of Tevet, derives spiritual sustenance from the *keshet* of Kislev in order to withstand the powers of evil that are especially strong during that month. According to the *Sefat Emet,* this influence is indicated in the number of lights kindled during the entire eight-day Chanukah holiday—thirty-six. The six correspond to the six days of Chanukah that occur during Kislev; the other thirty illuminate the thirty days of Tevet.

The energy of Kislev is indicated clearly in that its element is fire, the first element in the four that correspond to the months. The fire element, according to astrology, is conducive to the power of rulership.

Shevat, whose sign is Aquarius (*dlee,* water pitcher), is a water sign. The flowing of water symbolizes the Oral tradition, the words that Moshe spoke, which became the fifth book, Deuteronomy. According to the Midrash, this book was begun during the month of Shevat (see *Pri Tzadik,* Shemot, Shevat). The great later development of the Oral tradition began with the victory of Chanukah.

The month of Adar, whose sign is Pisces (dagim, fishes), also a water sign, symbolizes the purely voluntary acceptance by the Jewish people of the Oral tradition following the miracle of Esther. Our Sages say, concerning the verse (Esther, ch. 9, v. 27), "The Jews established and accepted," that after the Jews observed the true greatness of their Sages, they willingly accepted the Oral tradition.

According to the *Sefer Yetzirah,* each month bears its own combination of the divine Name (Yod, Heh, Vav, Heh), which is derived from the acronym of the first or last letters of a phrase in

Scripture. From the particular combination and phrase of each month we may learn its deep inner significance.

The combination of the name for Kislev derives from the passage (Genesis, ch. 50, v. 1), "Vayishma yoshev ha'aretz Haknani"—"And the inhabitants of the land of Canaan heard"—Vav, Yod, Heh, Heh. The first two letters, Vav and Yod, are the giving, male letters, and the last two Hehs are the receiving, female letters. From this we derive the nature of the influence of Kislev on the months that follow it.

The relationship between giving and receiving is also evident in the name Chanukah, which is etymologically related to the word *chinuch* (pedagogy). Astrology also regards the Sagittarian as having a ripe pedagogic ability, as one who cares deeply about his fellow man and does not hold back his gifts. These traits become fully developed in the service of Torah and its ways. On the other hand, these pedagogic abilities, if not directed along the spiritual path, may result in the exercise of destructive impulses.

The great influence that Kislev has on the months that follow it is most clearly expressed in the letters of its sign, *keshet* (bow), from which the other signs are derived through permutations of the letters. The letters of the word *keshet* are all in the class of "hundreds" (Kuf, 100; Shin, 300; Tav, 400), whereas the letters of the signs of Capricorn (*gdee*) or Aquarius (*dlee*)—Gimel, 3; Daleth, 4; Yod, 10; Daleth, 4; Lamed, 30; Yod, 10—are either singular or in tens. According to Kabbalah, "hundreds" represent the highest created world, the world of Creation; "tens" represent the next level, the world of Formation; "singles" represent the lowest world, the world of action, where the light is most contracted.

Capricorn, the goat, is a symbol for Esau, as the *Zohar* (vol. 2, 185) and Nachmanides explain regarding the sacrifice of goats in the Temple. Nonetheless, it is still accepted as a sacrifice because of its power to convert evil to good (see *Shem MiShmuel* on Chanukah). According to the *Avnei Nezer* (see ibid.), this process of incorporation of evil into good is fouled, as it were, by the fact that the first days of Tevet are still incorporated within Chanukah, days of miracles that fulfilled the prophecy (Habakkuk, ch. 3, v. 13): "You smote the head of the house of iniquity."

The heavenly body that influences Sagittarius is Jupiter, the largest planet of the solar system, which, according to the *Sefer Yetzirah,* was formed by the letter Gimel after the formation of Saturn by means of the letter Beth. After Jupiter, Mars was formed by the letter Daleth. So, too, the sun was formed by the letter Chaf, Venus by the Peh, Mercury by the Resh, and the moon by the letter Tav.

The letter Gimel, which formed Jupiter, symbolizes *gedulah,* abundant grace and the granting of favor. This is the essence of the energy of Jupiter, called in Hebrew *Zedek* (righteousness).

In the body, the organ that corresponds to Kislev is the stomach, pointing to the relationship between overeating and sleep, the attribute of the month. Overeating may also result in coldness toward spiritual things. According to astrology, the Sagittarian has a strong desire for food and a tendency to overeat.

TEVET
Capricorn (Goat)

The month of Tevet was formed, according to the *Sefer Yetzi-rah,* by means of the letter Ayin. Its nature is anger; its sign is the mountain goat (*gdee*), Capricorn; its organ is the liver. The name Tevet indicates a lack of abundance of good influence, as the letter Vav—which would turn the word into Tovat, abundant goodness—is missing. Nonetheless, the word Tevet does have a connotation of light, from the word *hatava* (meaning preparation of the wick), referring to the light of Chanukah (see *Sefat Emet,* Chanukah).

Tevet is one of the months that belong to the evil influence (so to speak) and its hidden powers, as mentioned in the *Zohar* (vol. 2, 12a) on the passage (Exodus, ch. 2, v. 2): "She hid him for three months" (referring to Moses). It was during Tevet that the siege that eventually led to the destruction of Jerusalem began. During the month of Tammuz, the walls of the city were breached, and during Av the Temple was destroyed. Thus, those three months—Tevet, Tammuz, and Av—are said to be under evil influence.

The element earth, associated with Tevet, symbolizes the sluggish power of materiality that predominates this month's influence. On the other hand, it is within the earth that the power of sustenance of life is contained; this parallels the influence of the organ of the month, the liver, which is the source of fresh blood for the human body.

According to the Ari, the months Tevet and Shevat correspond to the two eyes. The eyes are the most sensitive organs in terms of their ability to draw a person away from spirituality: "The eye sees, and so the heart desires."

During the two summer months, the eyes correspond to the months Tammuz and Av, and thus parallel the two winter months Tevet and Shevat. The natural attribute of Tammuz is vision, which is dependent on the eye. This is where evil finds its first base of influence. The sign for Tammuz, *sartan* (crab) of Cancer contains the word *soten*—hostility—together with the letter Resh, signifying motion and fluctuation. According to Nachmanides, Tevet's sign—the goat—is associated with evil.

The heavenly body that influences Capricorn is *Shabtai* (Saturn). It etymologically symbolizes limitation and inactivity (*hashbatah*) and, thus, again leaves room for the destructive activity of the evil influence.

In its positive aspect, Saturn symbolizes the power of deep understanding and contemplation associated with the Sabbath—i.e., the refraining from mundane activity in order to experience the transcendental.

The negative expression of this sign is evidenced by its being a festive occasion for Christians when, in the course of history, much innocent Jewish blood was shed. Joseph Stalin, an extreme anti-Semite, was born under the sign of Capricorn, as was, according to Christian tradition, the founder of Christianity.

The tribe of this month is the tribe of Dan, symbolizing the power of severe judgment (*din*). That is, it signifies the power of Esau, which judges the Jewish people harshly, for their having forsaken the Torah and its ways. In the desert encampments of the Jewish people, the tribe of Dan was in the north, from whence issue darkness and judgment, the place in the world where the sun is in hiding, so to speak. The north is also associated with the amassing of material wealth. It was from there, the Midrash explains, that the tribe of Dan received the gold it contributed to the making of the Golden Calf. This is one of the meanings of the rabbinic proverb "Harotze sh'easher yatzpin" (he who wants wealth should hide himself)—"He who wants to attain wealth should face north."

Astrology relates that people born under the sign of Capricorn are strongly drawn to the desire to amass material wealth. This tendency is expressed in the letter Ayin, the letter of this month, as well as in the (right) eye, the facial organ of the month, according to the Ari. The negative pseudological aspect of the eye is that it lends itself to impatient ambition, and this acts as a complement to the brazenness of the mountain goat Capricorn (the Hebrew word for mountain goat, *gdee ezim,* is related to the word for the strength and fierceness, *ezuz*).

On the Jewish path, during this month one ought to pay special attention to the spiritual function of sight, as in the contexts of the verse (Isaiah, ch. 40, v. 26). "Lift your eyes on high and see; who created these." One should also note the correspondence of divine Providence of "The eye of God is inclined toward those in awe of him" (Psalms, ch. 33, v. 18). According to Rabbi Zaddok Hakohen, this form of service to the Divine derives its connection to the month of Tevet because of the month's emotive attribute *rogez* (anger), which has the same numerical value as the word *yira* (fear and awesome awareness). This helps one to direct one's energy of fierce anger against one's inclination to do evil. The word *rogez* is also numerically equivalent to the word *gevurah*—power (the first of the six sefirot of *Yetzirah* on the left side) to indicate the potential for rectifying this emotion in holiness.

Evil uses this month's power to overcome the holiness of Israel. The salvation of the various negative attributes of Tevet can bring a person great spiritual attainments and increases one's ability to function in the world, because of the downfall of the power of Esau—the power of evil.

This process is symbolically contained in the letter Ayin (ע), for, according to the *Otyot d'Rabbi Akiva,* Ayin symbolizes the power of Esau. Its crouched and bent form bespeaks the future downfall of Esau. This depends on the rectification of the sense of sight contained in the eye (the Hebrew word for eye is *ayin*), so that it stays clear of the evil influence.

Within the realm of holiness, the letter Ayin, with its numerical value of 70, denotes the seventy faces of the Torah— i.e., its seventy means of interpretation. Those who humble themselves before God merit this multivarious understanding; through it, one attains the power to subdue the evil influence of all the nations of the world.

The power of the wisdom of the Oral tradition became appreciated by the nation of Israel upon the downfall of the secular influence of Greek wisdom during Chanukah, which extends into Tevet for two days. The light of Chanukah is the hidden light, about which it is said (Psalms, ch. 31, v. 20), "O, how abundant is your goodness which you have hidden for those who fear you." The preparation (in Hebrew, *hatavah*) for this light occurs during the month of Tevet, as indicated in its name. By means of the hidden light, one nullifies the darkness and gross materiality of the north (the Hebrew word for "hidden" in the abovementioned verse is *tzafon,* related to the word for north, *tzafon*).

According to Rabbenu Bachaya, the nation associated with the sign of Capricorn is the Philistine nation. For this reason Samson, from the tribe of Dan, gave his Philistine wife a goat as a gift. He wanted to purify the evil influence of the Philstine at the root. The Philistines were always a problem for the Jewish people, and, as is stated in the books of Joshua and Judges, when Israel did evil in God's eyes, they were delivered into the hands of the Philistines.

The power of stern judgment within the Philistines is indicated in the numerical value of their name—860—which is ten times the divine name Elokim (86), the name that denotes judgment. Corresponding to this stands the tribe of Dan, at its head Samson, who wanted to put an end to their evil influence. However, the time was not yet ripe, for Israel had not yet achieved a high enough spiritual level. Perhaps the problems that Israel currently has with the Palestinians are a carry-over of the previous problems with the Philistines. (It is interesting to note that the PLO was founded, thirty years ago, during the month whose sign is Capricorn.) The solution to this problem is assured only by the return of the nation of Israel to walk in the ways of God and observe the Torah. Thereby, the negative influence of Capricorn will be transformed to the realm of holiness.

According to astrology, the sign of Capricorn influences both the Jewish and the Hindu nations. However, this negative influence extends to the Jews only if they fail to follow the ways of the Torah: Israel is above the constellations, since through devotional prayer and study it has the power to annul the power of the constellations.

During the month of Tevet, one ought to arouse within his heart intense fear and awe of God. *Pri Tzadik* (Genesis, Shevat) says that this power derives from Joseph, who said, "I fear the Lord (Elokim)" and "lest I sin to Elokim." The influence of Joseph is strongly felt during the month of Tevet, for on the Sabbaths of this month we read in the Torah the end of the story of Joseph's sojourn in Egypt.

The intense insecurity that Joseph must have felt at that time is, according to astrology, one of the character traits of the Capricorn, who is always looking for nurturance from people around him. The real nurturance is derived by following the spiritual path.

In Jewish practice, during the months of Tevet and Shevat, we read the first eight portions of the book of Exodus (abbreviated Shovevim Tat, for Shemot, Vaera, Bo, Beshalach, Yitro, Mishpatim, Teruma, and Tetzaveh). According to Kabbalah, this time is auspicious for correcting the sins of the covenant and adultery.

The difficult time of Tevet is mirrored in the Torah portions of the week, read on Shabbat, that discuss Israel's exile in Egypt and the tribulations suffered there. The power of Joseph the righteous, who corresponds on the side of holiness to the evil power of Esau, is strongly aroused during this time.

The drawing of the influence of Sagittarius (the bow, *keshet*) into Capricorn, through the power of Joseph, is effected during the holiday of Chanukah, whose days extend into Tevet. It is also noted in the symbol of Greece (the goat), as God said to Abraham at the covenant of the halved sacrifices, and as is noted in the prophecies of Daniel: that the subjugation of Israel to Greece is symbolized by the mountain goat. It was the power of the brazenness (*azut,* related to the word *ez,* goat) of evil that was revealed when the Greeks forced the sages of Israel to translate the Torah into the Greek language during the month of Tevet. This translation aroused great spiritual darkness for the Jewish people and was likened to the desecration of the Golden Calf. The darkness of Greece was extinguished by the light of Chanukah through the holy power of Joseph.

The goat, of the different kinds of cattle, is the first to advance when taken to pasture, as the Talmud states: "Why do the goats always lead the other herds of animals? Because this is the process of Creation." First there was darkness; then there was light. This process also revealed itself in history, when first the Greeks wanted to bring us to spiritual darkness, and then came the light of Chanukah, the light of the Torah.

This nature of the goat to try to be first is also a part of the Capricorn character. Yet brazenness on the part of holiness overcomes brazenness on the part of impurity. This month obligates a person to remove all of the stumbling blocks in his path to the spiritual life. The root of these stumbling blocks lies in the desecration of the mark of the covenant.

The great holiness available to the Capricorn is indicated in the numerical value of the word *gdee* (goat) (גדי), 17, the same as the numerical value of the word *tov* (goodness), and the same as the numerical value of the divine Name (Yod, Heh, Vav, Heh) when the Yod is given the value of 1 (instead of 10, by means of the aleph, yod, kof; 1, 10, 100 permutation). However, in its negative connotation it contains the same numerical value as the word *zvuv* (flying insect), which, according to Kabbalah, is associated with the impure manifestation of the level of *yesod,* the sign of the covenant. Goodness is the pure level of *yesod,* and the symbol of the *yesod* insect is its opposite (see *Zohar*, 128b, and *Kehilat Yaakov* on *zvuv*). *Zvuv* is the name of one of the fortified Philistine cities, named after their god of destruction. It is the negative manifestation of the power of Capricorn that wants to wound the holiness of Israel. This is indicated in the combination of letters that form the word P'leshet (פלשת), Shefal Tav (שפל-ת), the lowly base desires (Tav, according to the *Otyot d'Rabbi Akiva* symbolizes *taavah*, desire).

The evil of the Philistines is associated with Lilith, in the realm of desire (*Be'er Moshe* on 1 Samuel, 320); Delilah, whom Samson wanted to subdue, is a manifestation of that power (see the Ari's *Sefer Halikutim* on Judges). Lilith is the feminine manifestation of evil. This is clear from the name Delilah (דלילה), which in the A, Y, K; D, M, T permutation forms the name Lilith (לילית). Because of the low spiritual level of Israel during that time, instead of Samson subduing Delilah, she succeeded in temporarily subjugating him. The month of Tevet is set aside for subduing one's inclination in that direction, which is associated with the Philistines and the negative side of Capricorn.

According to the Midrash Tanhuma (Deuteronomy, Ha'azinu), the names of the astrological signs teach us about the process of the opening of the soul. The bow (Sagittarius) symbolizes the rising of the soul from Hell like an arrow sprung from above, as it is written in Zachariah (ch. 9, v. 13), "For I have shot Judah like from a bow." This prophecy refers to the war against the Greeks that preceded Chanukah. From that time on, Israel was made agile like a mountain goat who darts swiftly from rock to rock (see Shem MiShmuel, *Rosh Chodesh Tevet*, Chanukah).

The breaking forth of holiness during Chanukah attains its stabilization during Tevet, the time for *hatavah*, self-betterment and preparation for illumination. This process continues during the month of Shevat, whose letter is the Tzadi, symbolizing righteousness. The Ari associates Shevat with the eyes as well; it symbolizes the spiritual completeness of the eyes, as in the verse (Psalms, ch. 34, v. 16), "The eyes of God are inclined

toward the righteous." According to the *Kedushat Levi,* the letters Samech of Kislev, Ayin of Tevet, and Tzaddi of Shevat
symbolize the process of stabilization of the eyes in order to
ascertain righteousness (Samech, stabilization, stands for "sti-
mat ayin lirot bera"—closing the eyes and refraining from seeing evil: *ayin,* eye; Zaddi, righteousness). This process is
completed during the weeks of Shovevim Tat (the first eight
portions of Exodus). The main ingredient of the rectification is
the Oral tradition. This process began with Moses in the desert,
during the fortieth year, on the first day of the month of Shevat,
when he began Mishnah Torah, the review of the Torah
(Deuteronomy), which contains the roots of the Oral tradition.

The sign of the keshet (bow), symbolizing great strides in
holiness, is composed of letters in the "hundreds" position,
gdee (Capricorn) symbolizing contraction, and stabilization is
composed of "single" letters. The word *gdee* is also related to
the word *Eged* (binding together).

Tevet and its sign, Capricorn, symbolize many negative
traits in astrology. Those born under its influence have a tendency toward depression, seclusion, and loneliness. They feel
little satisfaction, and are angry at unfavorable circumstances—
the unfavorable results of their actions. These traits, derived
from the negative symbols of this month, are intended to draw
a person away from the mundane, to rectify his soul and
achieve satisfaction in the realm of the spiritual, as discussed
earlier.

The letters of the word *gdee* can be rearranged to form the
word *geed* (phallus), indicating the time of rectification. The
letter Yod in the word (Gimel, Yod, Daleth) symbolizes the
wisdom of the brain that produces the seed. It is placed between the Gimel and the Daleth to indicate the source of
energy being drawn forth and being imparted (*gomel dalim*—
gives to the poor). The misuse of the *geed* changes it into *gdee,*
where the Yod is removed from its rightful place. Placing the
Yod outside (instead of its being inside) attracts evil. The word
gdee, if permuted in the Aleph, Tav; Beth, Shin (first letter
changing with the last letter, second with second to last, etc.),

spells *keri* (nocturnal pollution), where the Yod is again on the outside. Thus, the numerical value of *gdee* (17), which is the same as *tov* (goodness), a symbol of the righteous *yesod,* indicates the internalization of the Yod, the rectification of the sign of the covenant. The *gdee* (Capricorn) energy, if used in the way of Torah, can bring goodness, but if not channeled properly, it leads to evil. This evil befell us as a result of the translation of the Torah into Greek, which brought on, many years later, the breaching of the walls of Jerusalem and the eventual destruction of the holy Temple, which occurred during the summer month that corresponds to the month of Tevet, the month of Tammuz, whose sign is *sartan* (Cancer).

The symbol of purity of *yesod* is the Tzadi, whose energy brought about the victory of Chanukah, and which rectifies the evil of Tevet. Joseph, the personification of *yesod,* is the holy correspondent to Esau, and does war with him (see *Siddur Beth Yaakov* of Rabbi Yaakov Emdem on Tevet). Joseph was born during Tammuz—Cancer. His relation to *keshet* (Sagittarius) is due, therefore, to lunar or planetary conjunctions. During Tammuz—which bodes evil, and which also corresponds to the eyes—was born Joseph, who overcomes the sensual temptations of sight that lead to adultery. The power to overcome this temptation is hidden in the souls of Israel, who are also called "the reminiscent of Joseph." Its exercise leads to the downfall of evil, and thereby the unhappy occasion that brought the days of fasting during Tevet and Tammuz will be turned to days of joy.

SHEVAT
Aquarius (Pitcher)

The process of unfolding the purity of the soul continues during the days of the sign of Aquarius (Midrash Tanhuma, Ha'azinu), following upon the softening of the soul during the time of Capricorn. The purification occurs by one's immersion into the waters of the Oral Torah, for the roots of this tradition are found in Moses's review of the Torah, which began on the first of Shevat. The Tzadi, symbolizing Zaddik (the righteous), is its letter, and its expressive nature is eating. Righteousness and eating are connected in the verse (Proverbs, ch. 13, v. 25), "The righteous one eats to the satisfaction of his body, but the belly of the wicked always feel empty."

The *Bnei Yisaschar* (Discourse on Shevat) says that, according to astrology, *dlee* (Aquarius) is the sign of the Jewish people, for although Israel is above the constellations, and although prayers and good works can obtain their true desire regardless of the determination of the constellations, their natural manifestation is associated with an astrological sign. Other astrological opinions say that Israel's sign is Capricorn. However, based on our previous statements, these two opinions may be reconciled. First, there may not be a contradiction at all, since Israel reckons astrology according to the lunar calendar, and the solar period of Capricorn often extends into Shevat, the lunar Aquarius. Also, as we have seen from the Ari, Tevet and

Shevat correspond to the two eyes, so there is a definite relation between these two months.

The *Sefer Yetzirah* relates that the stomach, where digestion occurs, is the bodily organ associated with *dlee* (Aquarius). The rectification of eating (this month's expressive nature) in holiness is essential to one's pursuit of righteousness (this month's letter, Tzadi). The level of the Tzadi is the natural level of Israel, as it is written (Isaiah, ch. 60, v. 21): "And your nation is entirely religious, they will inherit the land forever."

The bucket, *dlee,* is the sign of Israel because its sole purpose is to draw water, and water is a symbol for Torah, as it is written (Isaiah, ch. 55, v. 1): "Alas! All of you thirsty, come to the water." This indicates that Israel's essential purpose of Creation is to serve God through the Torah, and even if the judgment of the constellations issues decrees, one's work in the Torah and its laws shall turn it all to the good (*Bnei Yisaschar,* ibid.). The *Bnei Yisaschar* remarks, further, that because of Israel's rootedness in Aquarius, the water carrier, the sign of worthiness of the maiden destined to marry our Patriarch Isaac would be in the water carrier, as it is written (Genesis, ch. 24, v. 14): "And the maiden who upon my [Eliezer, the servant of Abraham] request for the water bucket shall say, 'Drink, and I will give also for your camels,' let her be the woman appointed by God to be for the son of my master." This is because it is a sign that the holy nation, whose sign is the water carrier, shall issue from her.

It was from this sign that Jethro, the father-in-law of Moses, a Midianite by birth and a man very wise in the science of astrology, discerned from the words of his daughters, "And he also drew water for us and gave the sheep water also" (Exodus, ch. 2, v. 19), that Moses was of the children of Israel, who do service through water.

Shevat, as a month that draws abundant blessings, is confirmed in the tribe that represents it, to whom the blessing was given (Genesis, ch. 49, v. 20), "As for Asher, fat is his produce." Fat (as in oil) is a symbol for Torah, for just as oil separates from other liquids and maintains its purity, so, too, is it with the wisdom of the Torah. Thus, both water and oil are used as symbols for Torah wisdom. *Shemen* (oil) is particularly a symbol for the Oral Torah (the Mishnah), which contains the same letters as *shemen*. The influence of the Oral Torah began to flow through Moses, who began Mishnah Torah, the review of the Torah on the first of Shevat. The Midrash Talpiyot relates that Asher stands at the opening passageway of Hell and does not permit entry to anyone who studied Mishnah, which contains the same letters as the word *shmena,* used in Jacob's blessing, "Me'Asher shmena lachmo"—"As for Asher, fat is his produce."

The element of the month of Shevat is air. Air is essential for the continued sustenance of the physical body. From this we may derive understanding about the special qualities of the month, which is the period of the beginning of the unfolding of the Oral tradition. The other months whose element is air are Sivan—when the Torah was given on Mount Sinai—and Tishrei, when the second set of tablets containing the Ten Commandments was issued. These three air signs revealed the light of Torah to the generation of Israel that wandered in the desert.

Keshet, Sagittarius, is a fire sign, and its letters are in the "hundreds" place. *Gdee,* an earth sign, has most of its letters of the numerical value of the "singular" place. *Dlee,* an air sign, has most of its letters in the numerical position of "tens." Adar, whose sign is Pisces, or *dagim* (fishes), a water sign and therefore close to earth, has letters in both "tens" and "singular" positions if we include the letter Mem (*dagim,* plural, instead of *dag,* singular), whose meaning is water.

The task of the Jew in this world is to draw from the wisdom of the Torah and to give drink to the rest of the world. This task was performed, even before the birth of Abraham's son Isaac, by Abraham's servant Eliezer of Damascus, the letters of which indicate his being *doleh umashkeh*—drawing water and giving drink to the world from the Torah of the Patriarch Abraham. The letters of the word *dlee,* when multiplied by ten, form the word *meshek,* the root of the word *mashkeh* (giving drink). The availability of these spiritual waters occurs upon the rectification of *gdee,* Capricorn, which symbolizes the phallus, the physical source of life.

Moses embodied the sign of Aquarius when he drew from the wellsprings of Torah and gave drink to the children of Israel. This quality is indicated in his name, Moses, whose letters in the Aleph, Yod, Kof permutation spell the word *doleh* (משה—דלה), drawing forth.

Moses (related to the word *moshiach,* or savior) saved Israel from the waters of the Sea of Reeds and later drew for them the waters of the Torah, during the month of the water carrier, Shevat. The connection of Moses to the month of Shevat is indicated—according to the *Bnei Yisaschar*—in the numerical value of this month's name: 311, the same as the word *ish* (man), as in the appellation, "ha'ish Moshe" ("the man, Moses") (Exodus, ch. 11, v. 3). The letters of the word *ish*— Aleph, Yod, Shin—signify the source of effluence. The Aleph, containing the same letters as the word *peleh,* symbolizes the *peleh elyon* (אלף—פלא)—the supernal wonder (mystery), the source of the crown (the first divine attribute, which mediates between the transcendent and the imminent); the Yod symbolizes the attribute of wisdom; and the Shin, with its three prongs, indicates knowledge and its natural application. The letters of the word *ish* (איש) also form an acronym for the three divine Names: Aleph, Heh, Yod, Heh; Yod, Heh, Vav, Heh; and Shin, Daleth, Yod. Kabbalah associates all three names with Moses; Aleph, Heh, Yod, Heh was revealed to Moses in Egypt: "I am that I am." (Exodus, ch. 3, v. 14). The name Yod, Heh, Vav, Heh, when fully spelled with Alephs (Yod, Vav, Daleth, Heh, Aleph, Vav, Aleph, Vav, Heh, Aleph), has the numerical value 45—Mem and Heh, two of the letters in the name Moses. The name Shaddai, when found together with the name El (א-ל—ש-די), as often found in Scripture, has the numerical value of 345, the same as the name Moses.

One of the names of Moses is *tov* (good), for when he was born it was noted that he was already circumcised (see Midrash Rabbah, Exodus, ch. 2, v. 1), as it is written (ibid.), "And she saw him and, behold, he was good." The precedence of Tevet—related to the word *tov,* and to the phallus—to the month of Shevat indicates the wholeness of the sign of the covenant, *yesod,* an essential attribute for the attainment of the effluence of Torah. Moses, complete in this attribute, received the Torah and gave it to Israel. The process of development of this wellspring unfolds for the spiritual benefit of Israel during these months, when the Sabbaths of reading the portions Shovevim Tat occur.

The heavenly body that influences Aquarius is Saturn (*Shabtai*). It also influences the sign of Capricorn. This means that it is a time for contemplation, for Saturn excels in its influence on understanding, and thus is conducive for an impartial review of one's life and repentance from the depths of one's heart. The letters forming the acronym Shovevim indicate that repentance depends on deep self-understanding and refraining from repeating one's mistakes. The *Zerah Kodesh* (Exodus) says that the numerical value of Shovevim, 360, the same as the acronym Shas (Shesh Sederot, the six orders of the Mishnah), indicates that an essential part of repentance for sins of the flesh is the process of deep investigation of the Oral tradition.

According to astrology, those born under the influence of *Dlee,* Aquarius, reveal a talent for originality and possess boundless inquisitiveness. Many scientists, including Copernicus and Galileo, have been Aquarians.

The connotation of filling oneself with the waters of Torah, which this sign contains, came to expression in the history of the Jewish people. This is particularly true of the Oral tradition. The main attributes of the Oral tradition are symbolized in the letter of the month, the Tzadi, whose form consists of the combination of the letters Yod and Nun, symbolizing wisdom and understanding (see *Pri Tzadik,* Exodus, Shevat).

The Yod and the Nun also symbolize the essential unity of the written and Oral traditions: the Yod, symbolizing wisdom, stands for the written Torah, and the Nun, symbolizing understanding, stands for the Oral Torah.

Wisdom and understanding always operate together. This idea is symbolized by the fact that the first renewal of growth in trees is discernible during the month of Shevat. The tree symbolizes the written Torah, and its fruit symbolizes the Oral tradition, which draws its sustenance from the written Torah just as a fruit draws sustenance from the tree. Here we find a clear example of how the physical parallels the spiritual (see *Chidushei HaRim,* Tu b'Shevat). According to the *Chidushei HaRim* (ibid.), the name Shevat is related to the word *shofet* (judge), because during this month one receives divine judgment on the spiritual sustenance of the whole year, for the capacity of originality in understanding the Oral tradition. This parallels the fact that the fifteenth of Shevat is the new year's day fortress, when the judgment on the quality and quantity of the next year's produce is divinely ordained.

The fact that this month is the source of inspiration for new ideas in the Torah may also explain the astrological prognostication that Aquarians are creative, because of the principle that when the wellsprings are opened they flow in two directions: to the spiritual wisdom of the Torah, and to the natural wisdom of the sciences. In fact, the *Zohar* predicted that there would be a great opening of the wellsprings of wisdom continuing from the year Tav Resh (1840 C.E.) onward. Beginning at that time, we noticed a significant increase of wisdom, both spiritual and secular. The name Shevat is also related to the word *poshet* (פשט), meaning spreading out, which denotes the spread of the influence of wisdom during the month of Shevat.

The period of Shevat, including its conduciveness for original thought, is indicated in the letters of its sign, *dlee* (דלי), containing the same letters as the word *yeled,* or *yoled* (ילד), "giving birth," and "the child," both indicating creativity. "The fruit of the righteous (*Zaddik*) is a tree of life" (Proverbs, ch. 1, v. 30). This passage expresses the implications of the month of Shevat: The Tzadi, the letter of the month, symbolizes righteousness; the fruit points to the fifteenth day of the month, when the first buds of the new fruit appear; and the tree of life symbolizes the Torah.

According to the Pesikta Zutrati (Exodus, Bo, ch. 24), the etymological implication of the name Shevat is from the word *shevatim,* the staff that afflicts, because it was during this month that God began afflicting the Egyptians with plagues through the staff of Moses. Each plague lasted a week (see also Midrash Rabbah, ch. 9).

According to the Midrash Rabbah and Tanhuma (Shemot), as well as the Mishnah (Tractate *Eduyot,* ch. 2), each plague lasted a month, and the last three plagues, which led to the downfall of Egypt, began during Shevat. These three plagues are associated with the attributes of understanding, wisdom, and the crown (see *Pri Tzadik,* Shemot, beginning of Bo). This is also indicated in the verse "Shevet lego kesilim"—"The staff strikes the fool," because it was only with the last three plagues that the proud and foolish King Pharaoh began to relent. Thus, the plague corresponding to understanding is locusts. With the decimation of Egyptian crops, an understanding began to enter the basely materialistic mind of Pharaoh. Understanding implies penetrating the veil of materials to discern what lies deeper. This is the function of the planet *Shabtai* (Saturn), etymologically related to the word *hashbata*—refraining from the mundane in order to gain perspective, related to the Sabbath, when the power of understanding is particularly evident.

Because the sanctity of the Sabbath is associated with the planet *Shabtai,* Rabbi Jonathan Eybeshitz explains, the nations of the world chose another day as their day of rest. The nation of Israel, which stands above the constellations, rests on the Sabbath, and merits deep understanding because of the extra portion of the soul given to us on the Sabbath.

As mentioned earlier, three months are regarded as being in the domain of Esau, or evil (see Shem MiShmuel, *Shemot,* Va'erah): The months of Tevet and Tammuz, and the first half of Shevat and of Av. The change occurs on the fifteenth of Av, which is regarded as a holiday because many joyous occurrences happened then, and the day became symbolic of renewal. On that day, the decree against the twelve tribes' intermarrying was lifted, and the tribe of Benjamin was allowed to marry into any other tribe. The fifteenth of Av also signaled an end to the time of tribulation in the desert, because on that day ended the death of those who did not enter the land.

Corresponding to the month of Av, the fifth of the summer months, is the month of Shevat, the fifth of the winter months. On the fifteenth of Shevat the trees start to bloom again after the long, hard winter. In a spiritual sense, this period marks the end of the influence of Esau, which began with the month of Tevet.

The change that occurs during the second half of Av and Shevat expresses itself in the combination of letters that form the divine Name appropriate for these months. The combination for Av is Heh, Vav, Yod, Heh, which symbolizes divine judgment, as it is written, "Behold the hand of God is upon thy cattle" (Exodus, ch. 9, v. 3), where the word *hoyah* (is upon) appears.

The beginning of the name for the month—Heh, Vav—contains the letters not in their natural order; the order in the name has the Vav before the Heh, whereas here the Heh precedes the Vav, a symbol of judgment. The last two letters—Yod, Heh—are in their correct order to indicate that the last two weeks of the month contain the influence of divine compassion.

The combination of the divine Name associated with Shevat is Heh, Yod, Vav, Heh. Here, too, the first two letters—Heh, Yod—are in the inverted order, symbolizing judgment, and the last two letters—Vav, Heh—are in a correct order, symbolizing the influence of divine compassion.

The fifteenth of Av, during the summer, and the fifteenth of Shevat, during the winter, complement one another. They signal the coming of a new era of rebuilding and development anticipating a new year (Av before Tishrei, Shevat before Nissan). Both are forty-five days before the New Year. Forty-five is the numerical value of the word *adam* (man). This tells us that for the forty-five days before the coming of the New Year, a person is given the energy to reconstruct himself along more Godly lines. In the Talmud (Tractate *Rosh Hashana*, 10b), we find that Rabbi Eliezer is of the opinion that the beginning of Creation occurred on the twenty-fifth of Elul; Rabbi Yehoshua holds that it began on the twenty-fifth of Adar. Thus, between the fifteenth of the month and the beginning of Creation is a space of forty days. This time period corresponds to the forty days from the time of conception that the embryo is formed in the womb (see *Bnei Yisaschar,* months of Tammuz and Av).

The month of Shevat is a time when anybody, no matter how far he is from holiness, may easily come closer to God and renew himself by detaching himself from his sinful past (Shem MiShmuel, *Shemot,* Va'erah). Similar prognostications are made by the science of astrology for those born under the sign of Aquarius, who note the energy of fundamental change, a clear break from the past.

In the context of Judaism, these qualities need to bring a person to spiritual renewal, to complete repentance and his liberation from the misdeeds of the past.

The difference between the two halves of the month is also seen in the tribe representing it, Asher, whose land is blessed with olives and oil. According to our Sages, olives eaten alone may sometimes cause forgetfulness, whereas olive oil is good for reinforcing the memory. The difference between the olive and the oil is that the oil is made by squeezing and grinding the olive. Similarly, during the month of Shevat, a person may undergo a fundamental change as a result of doing penance after the days of Shovevim, which are set aside for repentance. According to the *Zohar,* the tribe of the month is the tribe of Joseph, whose righteousness is confirmed in the letter by which the month was formed, the Tzadi.

According to modern astrology, both Saturn and Uranus influence Aquarius. In the process of the conscious unfolding of the divine attributes by man, the attribute of Uranus, which symbolizes wisdom, unfolds after the attribute of Saturn, understanding. Uranus corresponds to the right side of the tree of life, which consists of the attributes wisdom and grace; Saturn belongs to the left side, which consists of the attributes understanding and power (judgment).

On the path of Judaism, the rule over the sign of Shevat comes to expression in the combination of the divine Name for the month, which symbolizes the balance of grace and judgment. This is also the case in the month of Av, which is under the influence of the sun. The sun contains two qualities: the element of fire, which burns and darkens, and the quality of light and warmth. The month of Av also achieves its balance in the balance of judgment and grace implicit in the combination of the divine Name for that month.

The intermingling influence of the planets of wisdom and understanding in the month of Shevat points to its being a time for spiritual renewal, whose fullness is achieved by one's observance of the ways of the Torah.

The pursuit of holiness through eating, the main form of divine service for this month, in the form of "the righteous man to the satisfaction of his body," is the beginning of the process of divine service that culminates during the month of Nissan with the holiday of Passover, when the ritual eating of the paschal sacrifice and the matzoh (unleavened bread) takes place.

The tie that marks the inception of eating new fruits in ritual purity is the fifteenth of Shevat, the new year for fruit-bearing trees. The Hebrew word for tree, *ilan,* contains the numerical value of 91, symbolizing the balance of judgment, contained in the divine Name A-donai, with the numerical value of 65, and the divine Name Yod, Heh, Vav, Heh, symbolizing grace and mercy, and containing the numerical value of 26. Together, these two names have the numerical value of 91.

The unification of judgment and grace on the fifteenth day of Shevat (the new year for fruit-bearing trees) denotes the rectification of the sin of eating of the tree of knowledge. The eating of the fruit of this tree brought about a hiding of the divine Providence, with the separation of the world of action—the material world—denoted by the divine Name A-donai, from its supernal source, the spiritual world denoted by the divine Name Yod, Heh, Vav, Heh. It enabled the physical sciences to come to conclusions and deny the divine Providence. However, in time, the development of the physical sciences will reach a point at which the divine roots of the physical world will again be uncovered, as the *Zohar* states, on the verse "in the six-hundredth year of the life of Noah" (Genesis, ch. 7, v. 11): "In the six-hundredth year of the sixth thousand, the well-springs of wisdom will be opened both above and below. Then the world will be able to look forward to the day that is all peaceful and restful, just as on the sixth day of the week a man looks forward to the holy Sabbath." A person born during the month of Shevat has a natural aptitude for the physical sciences, according to astrology, and this pursuit will eventually lead him to true faith (*emunah*). The root of the word *emunah—amen—* shares the numerical value of 91 with the word *ilan* (fruit-bearing tree).

The powers of wisdom and understanding are the foundation of the attribute of knowledge. These powers are associated with the two ruling planets of Shevat, Saturn and Uranus, and will be wholly rectified through the tree of life, the Torah, and particularly through the Oral tradition, whose beginnings are to be found in the month of Shevat with the teachings of Moses, who reviewed the Torah at the end of the fortieth year of wandering in the desert.

The power of wisdom and understanding will bring a rectification to the tree that unifies grace and judgment, which issue forth from wisdom and understanding.

According to the science of astrology, those born under the influence of Cancer are deeply influenced and affected by their surroundings. The negative effects of this sensitivity are excessive fright and worry, which causes a desire to escape from grounded reality, because of a lack of self-confidence. In Jewish history, this was the chief cause of the tone of the spies' report. It also brought about the sin of the Golden Calf, for when the Jewish people mistook Moses as dead, they felt a severe lack of confidence in their future. Therefore, the Sages say in the Midrash, had it not been for the feeling of insecurity among the Jewish people, the astrological signs would not have had any negative influence on them.

On the positive side of the astrological influence, the sense of sight brings about a person's awareness of his neighbor, so that people can take an active interest in mutual well-being. The word for sight, *reiyah* (with an Aleph), has a homonym, *reiyah* (with an Ayin), which means caring for one's flock. This all depends on the sensitive and concerned merging of the Aleph and the Ayin, for the word (without vowels) *roeh,* with an Aleph, (seer), can also spell *raah,* (with an Ayin), evil.

The month's association with Reuben is connected with this, for Reuben was sensitive to the plight of his brother Joseph and tried to save him. He also felt the neglect of his mother, Leah, and tried to remedy that situation when he protested, after the passing of Rachel, that his father Jacob moved his tent to Rachel's concubine's quarters rather than to Leah's quarters, In the desert, the tribe of Reuben had a large flock of sheep.

Astrology describes the person under Cancer's influence as having a strong desire to care for his friends and loved ones. Reuben, however, was a bit rash in his defense of his mother, and, when he was involved in saving Joseph from his brothers, he did not think the situation through to its logical conclusion. This same rashness brought about the tribe of Reuben's quick acceptance of the claims of revolt of Korach against Moses; it also brought about the sins of the spies and the Golden Calf, when the Jewish people jumped to conclusions too quickly.

The winter month that corresponds to Tammuz is Tevet (the גדי, goat), which, according to the *Zohar,* is in the domain of Esau as well. We also find that the tenth day of Tevet, when the enemy invaded Jerusalem, corresponds to the seventeenth of Tammuz.

This correspondence is discussed in depth in many of the holy books. The books explain that when a person has control over his faculty of sight, so that it does not leave the realm of holiness, the energy of evil cannot have control over his person and his environment. This is the reason given for the fact that when the holy Temple was situated in Shiloh, the sacrifices were allowed to be eaten throughout the domain of the tribe of Joseph, for Joseph the righteous one protected the sanctity of the sacrifice from impure ingestion. This, however, was not the case when the Temple was moved to Jerusalem, where the sacrifices were allowed to be eaten only within the walls of the city. Joseph merited this distinction (he is referred to in Jacob's blessings as being "a fruitful vine by a fountain") because he did not allow his evil surroundings to penetrate beyond his field of vision.

The month of Tammuz, the month of sight, was blemished by the sins of the Golden Calf and the spies. This blemish of sight led, twelve centuries later, to the holy Torah's being seen by the Hellenists, who demanded translation into Greek in a non-sacred way. This, according to our Sages, was a violation on par with the Golden Calf. The translation (done by the Sages of the time, under great duress) was completed during the month of Tevet. So, too, our enemies, centuries later, surrounded the walls of the holy city of Jerusalem on the tenth of Tevet.

The letter that formed the month of Tevet is the Ayin (ע), and the meaning of the word *ayin* is eye, the vessel for the sense of sight, which is the essential attribute of the month of Tammuz. The letter that formed the month of Tammuz, the Heth (ח) denotes the twofold use of one's energy for *haim* (life) or for *het* (its opposite, sinfulness and destructiveness).

ADAR
Pisces (Fishes)

The sign of Dagim (Pisces), which the *Sefer Yetzirah* designates for the month of Adar, was formed by means of the letter Kof, with the emotional attribute of merriment. Its corresponding bodily organ is the spleen, and the combination of the divine Name for the month is Heh, Heh, Yod, Vav.

According to the Talmud (Tractate *Shabbat,* 102a), the letter Kof symbolizes *kedusha,* sanctity. In the Hebrew aleph-beth, it comes after the letter Tzadi, symbolizing righteousness. The level of sanctity is spiritually above the level of righteousness because the righteous one is still involved in the battle against his evil inclination, which he constantly subdues, whereas the sanctified one has successfully transformed his evil inclination to the good. It is this process that is implied by the ordering of the months—first Shevat, and then Adar.

During Shevat, a person measures up to his evil inclination in the form of the righteous one who eats to sustain his body; during Adar, whose most outstanding feature is Purim, the person attains the summit of holiness through feasting and merriment to the point beyond self-knowledge. Knowledge and perception, whose center of revelation occurs during the month of Shevat on the New Year of fruit-bearing trees, are thus transcended during the month of Adar.

The month of Adar marks the end of the six winter months and corresponds to Elul, the sixth of summer months. This correspondence is mirrored in the letters that form the nature of these signs: Adar was formed by the Kof, whose numerical value is 100, while Elul was formed by the Yod, whose numerical value is 10. Each represents completeness in its domain; 100 is the completeness of the "tenth" place, and 10 is the completeness of the "singular."

The letter Kof, as explained in the *Zohar* (vol. 2, 148b), represents the posture of imitation, like a *kof* (monkey) imitating a man. This posture in the positive sense implies the imitation of the ways of God, where in its negative sense it represents the conformist imitation of evil. Thus, in the Talmud and the *Zohar,* when discussing the spiritual implications of the letter Kof, the Talmud talks of its positive aspect—the imitation of God's transcendent sanctity—and the *Zohar* talks of its negative aspect—the monkey imitating the man. This negative imitation is exemplified by the tribe of Amalek, whose letters spell *amal kof,* the mischief of the monkey.

On Purim, the evil of Amalek is personified in Haman, the persecutor of the Jews. His fall, which occurred during Adar, due to the merit of repentance on the part of the Jewish people, brought the letter Kof into the realm of holiness. The posture of imitation that characterizes this month is at the root of the Jewish custom of dressing in masquerade during Purim.

Laughter and merriment are the highest expressions of joy and gladness. Under usual circumstances, they are forbidden in this world (see the Talmud, Tractate *Berachot,* 31a), even in the process of performing a *mitzvah,* a positive deed (see *Pri Tzadik,* Shemot, Rosh Chodesh Adar).

According to astrology, the Piscean personality is very flexible and can easily adapt to change or bring about a change in himself. He is, therefore, able to associate with various types of people. He has the type of personality that makes for a superb actor. Astrology ascribes this trait to Pisces being the last in the wheel of signs, and, therefore, represents the highest stage of development; the Piscean personality is free of the constraints of material manifestation and can, therefore, change easily.

In Judaism, the great power of Pisces reveals itself in the festival of Purim. In the days of Mordechai and Esther, the Jews underwent a deep change, which resulted in their acceptance of the Torah out of love of God, as the Talmud remarks on the verse (Esther, ch. 9, v. 27), "The Jews upheld and accepted," the Jews then willingly accepted the ways of the Torah (see Tractate *Megilla*, 7a). Since that time, the spiritual power of the Jews came to be ascendant during that month, and the experience of oppression under foreign domination became diminished. The ascendancy into holiness is marked by the Purim feast, when the Jew reaches holiness that surpasses understanding.

The letter Kof, according to the *Otyot d'Rabbi Akiva*, is associated with Moses, who was *makif*, or encompassed the wisdom of all of the wise men of Egypt with his own. Moses was born, and passed away, during the month of Adar, the month associated with the letter Kof. The level of Moses, who personified the levels of wisdom and understanding, was attained by Mordechai the righteous, who formed the process whereby the Jews willingly accepted the Torah in the days of Purim. This acceptance referred primarily to the manifestation and process of the Oral tradition, which, according to the Midrash Tanhuma (Noah), the Jews were not in full consent about when they accepted the Torah from Moses. Only upon recognizing the sublime spiritual stature of the Sages during the time of Purim (when Mordechai was highly instrumental in effecting the salvation of the Jewish people, which was highly imperiled) did the Jews willingly accept the authority of the Sages.

The sign of this month, Pisces, symbolizes both the nation of Israel and the Torah, for just as the fish is at home only in the water, where his whole life is spent, so, too, the Jew is only entirely at home when he conducts his life in the ways of the Torah, which transforms a life that awaits death to a life of sanctity. The two fishes of Pisces stand for the written and Oral aspects of the Torah. This corresponds to the sign of the month of Sivan, Gemini (twins), whose double form also symbolizes the written and Oral Torah.

According to the Gaon of Vilna (commentary of *Sefer Yetzirah,* ch. 8, Mishnah 9), Adar, the sixth of the winter months, symbolizes the sixth millennium, when God will make a circle dance with the righteous, when He will visit retribution on the evil of the nations of the world, with Gog the rebellious at their head, as the verse states (Psalms, ch. 2, v. 4), "He who sits in heaven is laughing, God has them in derision." At that time the earth will be filled with spiritual wisdom, as the prophet states (Isaiah, ch. 11, v. 9), "The earth will then be filled with the knowledge of God as the water covers the sea." This is the meaning of the water symbol associated with Pisces. The element of this month also is water, symbolizing the effluence of the Torah, which flows with living waters.

The sign of Pisces marks a sublime period in the Jewish calendar, when man, through the power of his soul, comes to transcend the level of corporeality. This is echoed in astrology, which assigns to the Piscean personality the characteristic of wanting to escape from the material plane, from discrete manifest existence. In its negative aspect, this tendency may express itself in alcoholism and drug abuse. In Judaism, this tendency reaches its spiritual climax during Purim, when a person, through indulging in eating and drinking in performance of a mitzvah (a positive commandment), becomes utterly sanctified.

Similarly, this is seen in the posture of imitation associated with the Kof, the letter of the month, indicating the limitation of the sacred, which reaches its climax in the merriment of Purim. Normally, imitation may bring a person to deceitful impersonation and lying. In fact, astrology regards these as the chief pitfalls of the Piscean personality.

Symbolizing the sign of Adar are two fishes, who are facing away from each other. The astrological explanation for this is that one fish is facing in the direction of the sign of Aquarius, symbolizing the desire for complete self-rectification in the material realm; the other fish faces Aries, symbolizing the desire to transcend one's material surroundings and attain spiritual awakening. One fish represents wholeness on the physical plane; the other fish represents the everlastingness of the soul.

In Judaism, the two fishes symbolize Mordechai and Esther, who, in their righteousness and purity (symbolized by water), brought unity to the Jewish people and brought them (Esther, ch. 8, v. 16) "light and gladness and joy and honor."

Mordechai and Esther, the liberators of the Jewish people in the historical period of Purim, contain in the first letters of their names the letter Aleph and Mem spelling the word *em*— mother. These are also the first letters of the redeemers of the Jews in Egypt, Moses and Aaron, as well as the first letters of the names of our future redeemers, Elijah the prophet and the Messiah (see *Mincha Belulah,* beginning of Behukotai).

This also explains the relationship between the months of Adar and Sivan, Pisces and Gemini, both symbolized in the double form. The twins of Gemini (Sivan) symbolize Moses and Aaron, who liberated the Jews from Egyptian bondage and gave them the Torah during the month of Sivan. So, too, the two fishes of Pisces (Adar) symbolize Esther and Mordechai, who brought the Jews to accept the Torah out of love of God, after their liberation during the Persian exile. Mordechai, the Messiah, and Moses all bring to Israel the sublime enlightenment of the soul (symbolized by the fish, who is at home in the water); Esther, Aaron, and Elijah bring spiritual rectification to the soul so that it is prepared for the great divine light.

The element of water associated with the month of Adar denotes the flexibility of character that allows for profound change, as that which occurred to the Jewish people during Purim. The term *shoshanat Yaakov* (the rose of Jacob), used to describe the Jewish soul, indicates this potential for change, in Hebrew *shinui;* for, during the days of Mordechai and Esther in the Persian exile, the Jews changed their evil ways for the ways of the Torah.

This attribute of change also indicates the relationship between Adar, the sixth of the winter months, and Elul, the sixth of the summer months. Elul is also regarded by astrology as one of the "changing" months. The concept of change during Elul refers to the fact that the month of Elul is set aside as a time for repentance, in preparation for the High Holy Days in Tishrei, the month that follows it. The form of repentance stressed during Elul is the return to God out of love, indicated by the fact that the name Elul is an acronym for "Ani ledodi ve-dodi li"—"I am for my beloved and my beloved is for me."

Without the instruction of the Torah, the Piscean finds himself confused by an ambivalence that comes as a result of deep questioning. He feels both love and hate at the same time, which may bring about profound suffering. When informed by the Torah, Adar becomes a great month for the Jewish people.

The name Adar is related to the word *adir* (meaning nobility and power), and refers to the verse (Psalms, ch. 93, v. 4), "Adir bamarom Hashem"—"The Lord on high is mighty" (see *Chidushei Harim,* Adar). In this psalm, the evil of the world is symbolized by "the voices of the mighty water" (ibid.). The mighty nations who wanted to destroy the Jewish people brought upon themselves the revelation of the mighty God. The waters were transformed into the returning waters of penance, referred to in the verse (Lamentations, ch. 2, v. 19), "Pour out thy heart like water before the face of God" (see *Bereshith Rabbah,* ch. 2, section 4). The mighty waters also symbolize the nations of the world that seek to engulf the Jewish people, just as the waves of the sea seek to engulf the sandy shore. The sand of the beach is also a symbol for the Jewish people.

The waters of penance destroy the waters of impurity. This is another meaning of the significance of Pisces' being a water sign. Water symbolizes modesty and humbleness, for water always flows downward, seeking its natural level. For this reason the Torah is likened to water.

The element of water, as a symbol of humbleness and submission, revealed its nature when the Jews, during the days of Purim, submitted to the direction of Torah. This is also indicated in the letters that form the name Adar—Aleph, the *aluf* (master of the world) to whom the Daleth and the Resh (both meaning poor and humble) submitted. It was the attitude of submission that attracted to Israel the salvation of God. The letters of the name of the sign, *dag* (fish) also symbolize this process, the Daleth (poor) attracts the Gimel (benefactor).

Astrology associates the Piscean with physical fragility and sensitivity to the elements. This "poverty" in the material realm can return to strength (*adirut,* from Adar) through one's dedication to the spiritual path of Torah. This was borne out during the period of the sign of this month, in the days of Purim.

The part of the body associated with this month by astrology is the sole of the foot, the extremity of the human body. This "last" part of the body corresponds to the month of Adar, the last month of the year. The heel (in Hebrew, *akev*) is composed largely of dead flesh. This is borne out by the word formed by the letters immediately following those of the word *akev:* Ayin—Peh, Kof—Resh, Beth—Gimel, spelling the word *peger,* corpse. However, we know that the sole of the foot is most ticklish, which brings about laughter. So, too, the month of Adar, the last month of the year, has as its expressive motion, laughter. The negative expression of laughter and frivolity is expressive of the power of Amalek (*amal kof,* the mischief of the monkey): "The wicked man is arrogant; his name is buffoon" (Proverbs, ch. 21, v. 24). However, in the future liberation, "our months will be filled with laughter" (Psalms, ch. 126, v. 1). Because of its holiness, Israel merits joy and gladness during the holiday of Purim.

Laughter is permissible only when in the service of the most lofty levels of holiness. It is a form of expression reserved for the most righteous of people, as the Talmud states (Tractate *Berachot,* 9b), "Rav Beruno never ceased from laughter ever since he began to say the blessing over the future redemption before engaging in prayer." The condition of laughter flows naturally from one who has transcended the bonds of the physical plane. This level of transcendence is given to us during the holiday of Purim, the sign of Pisces and its proximity to the sign of Aries. The month marking our liberation from

Egyptian bondage calls to mind this association of the blessing of redemption that precedes prayer, which arouses joy and laughter.

According to the Ari, the portion of the face associated with the month of Adar is the nose, wherein is contained the sense of smell. This is echoed in the relation of both Mordechai and Esther to sweet-smelling spices. Mordechai is likened to myrrh (in Hebrew, *mordror*), and Esther is called in the Scroll of Esther by the name Hadassa—myrtle. The sense of smell is regarded as the most spiritual of the senses, giving pleasure to the soul. It has the power of reviving the spirit, which is why it is used in the ceremony marking the close of the Sabbath, when the "extra soul" of the Sabbath takes its leave. The soul is reassured by smelling the spice.

The tribe associated with the month of Adar is the tribe of Naftali, about whom It is said (Deuteronomy, ch. 33, v. 22): "Naftali is satisfied with favor." The sense of satisfaction with blessing comes as a result of the acceptance of the Torah out of love of God. It is aroused every year during Purim, when the Jewish nation reaffirms its willing acceptance of the Torah.

According to the *Kedushat Levi,* which, in associating the months of the year with the tribes of Israel, also includes the tribe of Levi, the month of Adar is associated with the tribe of Joseph. His two sons, Ephraim and Menashe, correspond to the first and second Adar (during a leap year, an extra month of Adar is added to the lunar year). Joshua, who is the progeny of Ephraim, son of Joseph, engaged in battle with the nation of Amalek. After him, both Saul and Mordechai, descendants of Benjamin, Joseph's brother, engaged Amalek in battle.

The sons of Joseph, Ephraim and Menashe, were blessed by Jacob with the symbol of fish: "Veyidgu larov"—"Let them grow in multitude in the midst of the land" (Genesis, ch. 48, v. 16). The Talmud explains the form of this blessing as follows: "Just as the evil eye has no power over fish, who, being covered by water are hidden from sight, so too it has no power over the progeny of Joseph" (*Berachot,* 20a). The nation of Israel, also called the remnant of Joseph, merits this blessing during the month of Adar, when it was saved from the evil eye of Haman. The evil Haman intended for us "was turned to the contrary, and the Jews ruled over those that hated them" (Esther, ch. 9, v. 1).

The second Adar has no sign associated with it, and therefore, according to Rabbi Ephraim (quoted by the Chidah), witchcraft has no power over a person born during this month. According to the *Bnei Yisaschar* (Discourse 1 on Adar), which quotes an ancient oral tradition, Haman's decree for the destruction of the Jews was set for the second Adar. Haman, according to the Ari, was the incarnation of the primal serpent and was a magician (in Hebrew, the word for serpent— *nachash*—is related to the word for malevolent magician, *menaches*), as characteristic of the Amalekite nation in general. God nullified his intention of destruction by causing the lot to be cast for the second Adar, which is not associated with an astrological sign and is therefore impervious to malevolent magical influence.

The heavenly body that rules over Pisces is Jupiter, the same planet that rules Sagittarius. During these two months, our Sages instituted two holidays, Chanukah and Purim, when the powers of deceit and evil that characterized Greece and Amalek stood in opposition to the righteousness (in Hebrew, Jupiter is *Zedek,* which means righteousness) of the Torah and were defeated. During Chanukah, the victory belonged to the righteousness (*Zedek,* Jupiter) of the Torah; during Purim, the victory belonged to the righteousness of Israel.

According to Kabbalah, *Zedek* (Jupiter) is associated with *tzedakah* (charity), the charitable contributions that support those who devote their entire lives to Torah and spirituality.

The *Zohar* associates the wounding of Jacob's thigh by the guardian spirit of Esau with the desire on the part of evil to end the financial support of the Torah, for just as the leg and thigh support the body so that it can stand upright, so, too, the benefactors of the study of Torah support the upright position of the nation of Israel. According to our Sages, both the right and left thighs were wounded by Esau's guardian spirit. The right thigh came to symbolize Purim, and the left, Chanukah. This is the source of the custom to increase the giving of charity during these two holidays.

Jupiter, the largest of the planets, was formed by means of the letter Gimel, according to the *Sefer Yetzirah;* the letter Gimel, associated with the word *gomel,* refers to benefaction. According to the Talmud (Tractate *Sabbath,* 156b), this was the ruling planet of our Patriarch Abraham, the pillar of grace and benevolence.

According to astrology, in the symbolism of the human body, the influence of the legs begins in the month of Sagittarius. The sign of Sagittarius symbolizes the thighs, and the sign of Pisces symbolizes the soles of the feet. Thus, the symbolism of the legs both begins and ends with the influence of Zedek (Jupiter), righteousness, indicating that the righteous person is the foundation of the world. It was this attribute that the guardian spirit of Esau wanted to injure in Jacob and his offspring.

According to the *Sefer Yetzirah,* the internal organ of the month of Adar, the spleen, is associated with the emotion of laughter. The Talmud echoes this in the expression, "The spleen laughs" (*Berachot,* 61b). Laughter is permitted only to a person who is bound with his supernal source, as the Talmud says (*Berachot,* 30b) regarding a certain person who was in a state of laughter while donning his prayer phylacteries (*tefillin*). The tefillin symbolize the supernal crown, the root of the soul, the source of laughter. Only when a person is bound to this root may he safely engage in laughter. It was this level that was reached on Purim when "the Jews had light and gladness and joy and honor" (Esther, ch. 8, v. 16).

Index

and origins of Chanukah,
    66–68

Rachel, 78–79, 80
Rainbow, and Sagittarius,
    74–78
Rashi, 2
Rashness, and Shevat, 106
Rectification, 29–30, 92–93,
    96, 105
  in Adar, 39, 113
  in Elul, 48, 50
  of senses, 49, 87–88
  of thought, 19, 30
Redemption, through Mes-
    siah, 55–56
Renewal, 47, 67–68
  in Shevat, 99–100, 103–
    104
Repentance, 37–38, 99, 103
  in Elul, 49–51, 114
Return to God, 31, 71
  in Elul, 47, 49–51, 114
Reuben, 35, 37–38, 106
  tribe of, 24, 39, 41
Revolts, by tribes. See Leader-
    ship
Righteousness, 70, 73, 91–93,
    109, 117
  in Shavat, 95–96, 100
Rod, in Shevat, 46
Rosh Hashanah, 55, 62–63
Royalty, associated with Av,
    45

Sabbath, and Saturn, 86, 98
Sacrifices, 82, 104, 106–107

Sages, 66, 111
Sagittarius. See Kislev
Samech (letter), 65–66, 68, 92
Samson, 88, 91
Sanctity, 109, 112
Saturn, 86
  influence of, 98, 99, 103,
    105
Scales, as judgment, 55–56
Sciences, 104–105
Scorpio. See Cheshvan
Scorpion, and flood, 60
Sea of Reeds, 13, 24
Seasons, relationships among,
    31, 38
Secrets. See Mysteries/secrets
Service, to God
  in Cheshvan, 22–24, 61–62
  in Elul, 51
  in Iyar, 19
  in Kislev, 65
  in Nissan, 30
  in Shevat, 104
  and tasks of Jews, 97
  in Tevet, 87, 90
Seven, symbolism of, 27
Sexual union, in Tishrei,
    53–54
Shavuot, and Chanukah, 76
Shevat/Aquarius (pitcher), 29,
    55, 80–81, 91–92, 95–107
  relation to other signs,
    45–46, 62–63, 109
Shimon, Rabbi bar Yochai,
    75, 78
Shin (letter), 72
Shoftim, reading of, 48

About the Author

Rabbi Matityahu Glazerson was born and educated in Israel. He studied at Medrashiat Noam in Pardes Chana, and at various yeshivot, including Kfar Chassidim, Ponievez, and Chevron. Today he is involved in teaching in a Kollel, and lecturing at various institutions, like Neve Yerushalayim, Ma'ayonot Yerushalayim, and Kol B'Rama. He is instrumental in paving a new way toward the instillment of Jewish values. Rabbi Glazerson is the author of many books including *The Secrets of the Haggadah; Torah, Light, and Healing: Mystical Insights into Healing based on the Hebrew Language; Music and Kabbalah;* and *Building Blocks of the Soul: Studies on the Letters and Words of the Hebrew Language.*